LAWRENCE BLOCK

AFTER THE FIRST DEATH

LAWRENCE BLOCK's novels range from the urban noir of Matthew Scudder (*Hope to Die*) to the urbane effervescence of Bernie Rhodenbarr (*The Burglar in the Rye*), while other characters include the globetrotting insomniac Evan Tanner (*Tanner On Ice*) and the introspective assassin Keller (*Hit List*). He has published articles and short fiction in *American Heritage*, *Redbook*, *Playboy*, *GQ*, and *The New York Times*, and has published several collections of short fiction in book form, the most recent being his *Collected Mystery Stories*. Block is a Grand Master of Mystery Writers of America. He has won the Edgar and Shamus awards four times and the Japanese Maltese Falcon award twice, as well as the Nero Wolfe award. In France, he has been proclaimed a Grand Maitre du Roman Noir and has twice been awarded the Societe 813 trophy. He has been a guest of honor at Bouchercon and at book fairs and mystery festivals in France, Australia, Italy, New Zealand and Spain, and, as if that were not enough, was presented with the key to the city of Muncie, Indiana. He is a past president of the Private Eye Writers of America and the Mystery Writers of America.

"Block's fiction is tense and energetic. His stories unfold smoothly and elegantly, with plenty of detail and rich characterization."
—*The Houston Chronicle*

"There is only one writer of mystery and detective fiction who comes close to replacing the irreplaceable John D. MacDonald. The writer is Lawrence Block." —Stephen King

AFTER THE FIRST DEATH

LAWRENCE BLOCK

ibooks
new york
www.ibooks.net

A Publication of ibooks, inc.

Copyright © 1969, 2002 Lawrence Block

An ibooks, inc. Book

Distributed by Simon & Schuster, Inc.
1230 Avenue of the Americas, New York, NY 10020

ibooks, inc.
24 West 25th Street
New York, NY 10010

The ibooks World Wide Web Site Address is:
http://www.ibooks.net

ISBN 0-7434-4507-4
First ibooks, inc. printing August 2002
10 9 8 7 6 5 4 3 2

Cover photograph
copyright © 2002 Corbis

Cover design by Eric Goodman

Printed in the U.S.A.

for
What's-Her-Name

AFTER THE FIRST DEATH

· 1 ·

I CAME UP OUT OF IT VERY SLOWLY. AT FIRST THERE WAS ONLY the simple awareness of existence. I was lying on my right side, my right arm bent oddly so that my head rested upon my wrist. There was a slight tingling sensation in the fingers of my right hand, as though the weight of my head was cutting off part of the circulation in that hand. My left arm was stretched out at my side. I left every part of me as it was, and I kept my eyes shut. If I moved, or opened my eyes, my head would ache. It would ache soon enough anyway, but if I could slide gently back into sleep I could postpone the headache. With more than the usual amount of luck I might even be able to sleep through the entire hangover. This had happened occasionally in the past, though not often.

I knew there would be a hangover, knew too that I had gone out and earned one, though I could not remember it. I could remember very little, actually. I did not know where I was, or how I had gotten there, or what day it was, nor was I particularly anxious to find out any of these things. I knew —although I did not remember—that I had been drinking. When I drink I get drunk, and when I get drunk I have massive blackouts during which I do things, for better or for worse, which I do not remember, for better or for worse.

Usually for worse.

I had been drinking. I had thought that I had given that

up, but evidently I had been wrong. I had been drinking, and I had gotten drunk, and I had blacked out, all according to the usual pattern, and if I moved or opened my eyes I would have a hangover, and I didn't want one. If I opened my eyes just a crack I could at least learn whether it was day or night, and I thought about this, and it occurred to me that learning whether it was day or night was not reward enough to balance the punishment of a headache. It occurred to me, too, that all of this thinking was dangerous. It got in the way of a return to sleep. I kept my eyes closed and I made my mind push each thought resolutely away, like a beach rebuffing one wave after another until the sea grew calm. One thought after another, one wave after another, push, push, and the dark curtain came mercifully down.

The second time, my right hand woke me. The tingling in the fingers had ceased entirely, and now the whole hand was quite stiff, with the immobile fingers feeling at least twice their usual diameter. I pulled my hand out from beneath my head and shook it foolishly in the air. Then I used the left hand to rub the right wrist, rubbing furiously at arteries and veins to restore circulation. My eyes were still closed. My head spun with idiot visions of gangrene and amputation. I rubbed my wrist, and after a long time the fingers began to tingle once again, and I was able with effort to clench and unclench them. The headache began then, a two-pronged affair, a dull pain emanating from the center of the forehead and a sharp stabbing pain at the base of the skull in back. I went on rubbing my hand and flexing the fingers, and eventually the tingling subsided and the hand felt as a hand is supposed to feel, although the wrist was slightly sore from the rubbing.

I was lying on top of a bed, uncovered. I was cold. I touched my body with my hands and found that I was naked. I still did not know where I was, other than that I was in bed, and I still did not know whether it was day or night, as I still had not opened my eyes. I thought that I might as well open my eyes, as I had the damned headache anyway, but I somehow did not get around to it.

Chunks of time went by. I moved my arms and legs, rolled over onto my back. A chain of shivers jolted me and a wave of nausea started up in the pit of my stomach. I could not seem to catch my breath. I opened my eyes. There were cracks in the ceiling. A lightbulb, hanging from the ceiling, glared fiercely at me. I tilted my head. There was a window above the foot of the bed. I could see daylight through it, backed by the wall of another building. Red brick, once-red brick, faded almost colorless by the years. It was day.

I sat up. Everything ached. I was naked and cold, and by the side of the grimy window through which I could see that it was day, by the side of the window, there was a chair. My clothing was piled upon the chair. I crawled to the foot of the bed and stretched out an arm for my clothing. I could not reach it at first. For some reason I did not walk from the bed to the chair, though that would have been the most logical way to get the clothing. For some reason I had to stay on the bed, as though it were an island in the raging sea and I would drown if I left it. I stretched out head-first upon the bed and reached out with both arms until I was able to pull my clothing from the chair piece by piece. I dropped one sock onto the floor but managed to bring all the other garments safely over the sea of floor and onto the island of bed.

My shirt and trousers were damp and sticky. I held my shirt in both hands and stared thoughtfully, stupidly, at it. Dark red stains. Sticky. I wondered if I had been drinking wine. Usually I drank whiskey, at least at the beginning, but once I was well into it, once I was past the point of no return, which happened often, and quite quickly, then I was apt to drink almost anything. And, once I reached a certain plateau of drunkenness, I was equally apt to spill whatever I had been drinking upon myself.

I touched one of the stains. It was not wine. I looked at it and smelled it and touched it again, and it was blood.

Had I been in a fight?

That was possible, of course. Anything was possible when I drank. Anything at all.

Had I been hurt? Once I had awakened quite like this to find myself tied to a bed, my feet tied to the foot of the bed, my hands to the headboard. I had been in a hospital, with no memory of being taken there and no idea of what was wrong with me. Very little, as it had turned out. I had cut myself and had been bleeding, but not that badly.

Had I had a nosebleed? I get nosebleeds frequently, especially when I drink. The alcohol dilates the small capillaries in the nose and makes them more easily ruptured. I investigated my nose carefully with both hands. There did not seem to be any blood around the nose or any blood caked inside the nostrils. I wondered idly where the blood might have come from.

I started to put on the shirt, then stopped suddenly, realizing that I could not possibly go anywhere in these horrible bloody clothes. Then how was I to get out of this place? Obviously, I would have to call someone on the telephone and have him bring around fresh clothes. But how? I didn't even know where I was. I couldn't even be sure what city I was in, as far as that went. Of course I might find out that much from the telephone, but I couldn't find out the address from the telephone. Or could I?

It was all a problem and I did not want to think about it. I looked at my hands. They were bloody from the clothes. I decided that I could not have slept very long, or else the blood on my clothes would have dried by now. I wondered how I could have gotten blood on my clothes. A nosebleed seemed unlikely. Had I been cut?

I investigated my body very carefully. Everything appeared to be sound and undamaged. Then how had the blood gotten on my clothes? Was it someone else's blood? If so, whose? And how had it gotten there?

I didn't care to think about all of this. I stretched out on the bed again, on my side again, and I closed my eyes. I would push away all thoughts, I thought again, like a beach rebuffing waves, and everything would be calm and dark again.

But it did not work. I could not even keep my eyes closed. I was awake, undeniably and irretrievably awake, and everything ached—my arms and legs, my back, my head, my stomach, everything. Nausea returned, stronger than before, and I only fought it off with a great effort.

I couldn't stay there. I had to get away. I had to find out where the hell I was, and I had to have someone bring clean clothes, and then I had to get dressed and go home. Had to.

I sat up on the bed and looked around. I was in a small room with the door closed. There was the one window I had seen before, and the single wooden chair, and a battered chest of drawers with innumerable cigarette burns on its otherwise empty top.

I started to get up, and there was something on the floor, something sticky that my feet touched.

Wet and sticky.

I closed my eyes. A shiver went through me, a chill caused by more than the cold and my own nakedness. I kept my eyes closed and folded my arms foolishly across my chest. I did not want to look. I did not want to know. I wanted to go to sleep and stay asleep for ages and wake up elsewhere, miles and years away.

I wondered, briefly, if it was a dream.

I opened my eyes again. I picked up one foot and looked hopelessly at the bottom of it. Blood. I tried to catch my breath, and somehow couldn't, and I looked at the floor, and the nausea came back again, in a flood, with no warning. I threw up with the spontaneity of the knee-jerk reflex. It was that automatic—I looked, I saw, I vomited. And did so repeatedly, long past the point where there was anything in my stomach to eliminate.

I thought of the way I had reached across the floor as if it were a sea in which I dared not set foot. An apt image. The floor was a sea of blood. A body floated upon this ocean. A girl; black hair, staring blue eyes, bloodless lips. Naked. Dead. Her throat slashed deeply.

It had to be a dream. It had to, had to be a dream. It was not a dream. It was not a dream at all.

I've done it again, I thought. Sweet Jesus, I've done it again. I believe I spoke the words aloud. And put my head in my hands, and closed my eyes, and laughed and cried and laughed and cried.

· 2 ·

IN THE YEARS WHEN I TAUGHT HISTORY (SURVEY OF WESTERN
Civilization, Europe Since Waterloo, Tudor and Stuart England, French Revolution and Napoleon) we made much of
historical imperatives, of the inevitability of virtually all major
developments from the fall of Rome to the Russian Revolution. I was never wholly convinced of the validity of this
viewpoint. I have since come to reject it utterly. History, I
suspect, is little more than the record of accident and coincidence and random chance. The English Reformation was
born in a lustful gleam in a regal eye. Presidents have fallen
to the lucky shots of madmen.

For want of a nail, says Mother Goose, a kingdom was lost.
And well I believe it.

Had there been a telephone in that room, I would have
dialed the operator and asked for the police, and they would
have come at once to take me away. There was no telephone
in the room. I looked, and there was none.

Had my clothes not been so thoroughly soaked with blood,
I would have dressed at once and left the building. I would
then have proceeded at once to the nearest telephone and
summoned the police, with the same results above described.
But my clothes were bloody, so very bloody that I could not
bring myself to put them on, let alone go anywhere in them. I
could barely summon up the strength to handle them.

Accidents, coincidences, chance. That there was no phone. That my clothes were bloody. That a Supreme Court ruling had released me from prison. That I had taken that unremembered first drink a day or a week or a month ago. That I had met the girl, and brought her here, and killed her. For want of a nail, for want of a nail.

I wanted a cigarette, I wanted a drink, I wanted to go away. My first reaction, to call the police, was temporarily stalemated. I had to do something. I couldn't stay where I was, in the room, with the girl, the dead girl. I had to do something. I had to get out of there.

There was a key on the floor by the side of the old dresser. An old-fashioned brass key attached by a piece of metal to a triangular wedge of pressed board a little longer than the key itself. HOTEL MAXFIELD, 324 WEST 49TH STREET, NEW YORK CITY. DROP IN ANY MAILBOX. WE PAY POSTAGE. The key itself was stamped with the number 402.

I was in a hotel. A cheap hotel, obviously, judging by the appearance of the room and the address of the hotel. A room, judging now by both the address and the body upon the floor, in one of those Times Square hotels to which streetwalkers take their clients. A room to which I had been taken and in which I had committed murder.

The headache grew more violent than ever. I covered my forehead with my hand and tried unsuccessfully to will the pain away. I took a step, slipped, and very nearly fell to the floor. I looked down and saw that I had slipped in the blood.

I turned my head so that I would not see the body or the blood. I walked carefully, skirting the blood, and got back to the bed. I sat on the bed and took the pillowslip from the pillow and used it to wipe the blood from my hands and feet. There were traces of blood elsewhere on my body and I got them off as well as I could with the pillowslip.

I stood up again and stripped one of the sheets from the bed. I folded it around me like a Roman toga and walked around blood and body once again and picked up the key and went to the door. It was latched. I slid the bolt back and eased the door open. The hallway, narrow and dark and dingy, was empty. I slipped out of the room and closed the door and locked it. The door did not have a spring lock; one had to lock it with the key. I walked down the hallway, feeling ridiculous in the improvised toga, hoping desperately that no one would appear. I found the communal bathroom—such hotels have communal bathrooms; I know much about such hotels, I have been in so many of them, so very many of them—and I entered the bathroom and shut and bolted the door. Someone had recently been sick in the toilet. I flushed it, and I closed my eyes, and opened them, and thought of the body on the floor of room 402—my room—and was sick again, and flushed the toilet a second time.

I filled the tub, after first washing it out carefully, and I seated myself in the full tub and bathed. The blood was my main concern. I had to get the blood off. Whatever I was going to do, I had to get the blood off me. I thought of Lady Macbeth. *Who would have thought the old man to have had so much blood in him?* So very much blood in one little girl.

When I got out of the tub I had nothing to dry myself with but the sheet. I used it and was left with nothing to wear. I looked at myself in the little fly-specked mirror over the sink. I did not seem to have more than a day's growth of beard. Then today was Sunday, I thought. The last thing that I remembered was Saturday, Saturday morning, and—

No. I was not yet ready to begin remembering things.

And it couldn't be very late. At those hotels, checkout time was generally somewhere between eleven a.m. and noon, although few of the guests stayed more than an hour or so. No one had come banging on my door, so it was probably still morning. Sunday morning.

I couldn't stay in the bathroom forever. I took my damp bedsheet and folded it neatly several times until it was the approximate size of a bath towel, then wrapped it around my waist and folded it upon itself so that it would hopefully stay in place without being held. I opened the bathroom door and saw a little old man walking down the hallway. I closed the door again. He passed the bathroom and continued on down the hall. When I heard his footsteps on the staircase I opened the door again, and this time the hallway was empty.

I went back to my room. There was no place else to go.

And it was there, in the room, perhaps half an hour after I had first looked for a telephone to summon the police, that I realized that I was not going to call the police at all.

I had been in prison for four years. *Inside,* my fellow prisoners called it (how they had despised me; they were criminals, professional or amateur criminals, and I was a woman-killer, and they loathed me for it). I had been inside for four years, and could look forward, according to the standard actuarial tables, to remaining inside for another thirty-seven years. I had become virtually resigned to it. It was not a good life inside. No one could say that it was. But it was a life of sorts, a life with pattern and regularity to it, a life even with the illusion of purpose, albeit the self-deceiving purpose of a hamster upon a treadmill. I had become resigned to it, and they should have left me there until I died.

That they did not was more my fault than theirs. Some damned guardhouse lawyer began making noises down in Florida. He submitted a brief to the Supreme Court, whereupon the Court made one of its landmark decisions. This took the stopper out of the bottle. I read that decision, and obtained a transcript of my own trial, and burrowed through law books, and discovered that my whole case now appeared to be a legal comedy. An unsubstantiated confession, lack of immediate criminal counsel, illicitly obtained evidence—a variety of crucial irregularities, unnoticed at the time, which now took on the shape of a passport to the outside world.

I could have let well enough alone. I was where I felt I belonged and could have remained there. But I was plugged into the machinery of liberation; like a driver so taken with the performance of his car that he misses his turn and drives on into the next county, the discovery of a way out caught me up completely. I was on the road, not stopping to wonder where it might lead.

My own legal action brought others in its wake. I kicked a hole in the prison wall and a handful of prisoners followed me through it. Our verdicts were set aside, and society had the option of releasing us or bringing us again to trial. Most of us could not be retried—evidence was gone or had never existed, witnesses had died or disappeared. And so we were set free, I and Turk Williams and a bank robber named Jaeckle and others whose names I have forgotten.

And now this girl was dead, and I couldn't go back. I could not do it, I could not go back, not now, not ever. I could not do it.

There was a knife on the floor. As far as I knew, I had never seen it before. But this did not mean much. As far as I knew I had not seen the girl before, or the room. I must have bought the knife Saturday afternoon, and I had evidently used it Saturday night. I could use it again. I could draw my own blood with it this time. I could slash my wrists. I could return to the tub and open my veins and bleed to death in warm water, like Cicero. Or cut my own throat as I had cut the throat of the girl. Wolfe Tone, jailed after the Irish Rebellion of 1798, had sawed through his throat with a penknife. I wondered if I could do the same. Would the hand falter? Would the pain surmount the determination? Or would purpose simply crumble halfway through the act, defeated by the will to live or the fear of death?

I never picked up the knife, never reached for it. I stood there, eyeing that knife, wanting a cigarette, wanting the knife, wanting to be dead. And merely thought about it.

I couldn't kill myself. Not now. I couldn't go to the police. And I couldn't stay in the room much longer. I simply couldn't do it.

I went through my trousers, being very careful not to get blood on my hands again. The pockets were empty. I was looking for cigarettes, and there weren't any, but while I was at it I looked for my wallet, and it was gone, too. This was no great surprise. Usually, after such a night as this had been, I would awaken without watch and wallet. Both were gone now, and it was no surprise. Evidently I had been rolled before I picked up the girl. Perhaps that was how it had happened, perhaps she had requested money and I had had no money and that was what provoked me. Perhaps—

No. I still didn't want to try remembering it. I didn't even want to speculate, not yet.

I just wanted to get out of there.

I went to the door again, opened it. The hotel was noisy now. The guests were waking up and getting out. I waited at the door, held it open no more than a crack, watching, waiting. A tall thin man walked beside a short thin Negro girl. His blond hair needed combing and his face was lined with exhaustion. He looked desperately ashamed of himself; she looked merely tired. They passed. A door opened and a very effeminate young man emerged from it and left. Moments later a sailor vacated the same room; his face held the same expression of shame and exhaustion that I had seen on the face of the tall blond man.

Finally, two doors down the hall, a man in a white terrycloth robe emerged from a room, crossed the hall, and entered the bathroom. He did not lock his door.

He was about my height, a little heavier. I slipped out of my room and locked my door and padded barefoot down the hall to the bathroom door. He was running water in the tub. He would be a while.

I went to his room, opened his door. I felt a moment's panic at the sound of footsteps in the hall, then realized that no one would know I was entering a room other than my own. I went inside, closed the door, slid the bolt home.

There were clean underwear and socks in the dresser. No clean shirt, so I took one from a hook in the closet, a plaid flannel shirt, slightly worn at the elbows. It was big on me.

He had only one pair of trousers, dark brown, wool, with pleats and cuffs. They were about four inches too big in the waist and very baggy in the seat, but by drawing his belt to the last notch they just about stayed up. The pants had buttons on the fly instead of a zipper. They were the first pair of pants with buttons on the fly that I had seen in more years than I could remember.

His shoes, unlike everything else, were too small. Heavy cordovan shoes, quite old-fashioned. The laces had been broken and retied. I squeezed my feet into them and tied them.

His wallet was in a drawer in the dresser. I didn't want it, or his National Maritime Union card, or his driver's license, or his condom. There were two one-dollar bills and a five in the wallet. I took the three bills, then hesitated, then put the two singles back. I stuffed the five into my pocket—his pocket, originally, but mine now, possession being nine points of the law and ten points of the truth—and I left his room and hurried back to my own.

I changed his belt for mine, and now the pants stayed up better. They still did not feel as though they had been designed with me in mind, but neither did the shirt or the shoes, and it hardly mattered.

It bothered me, stealing from a poor man. He would miss the clothes, the five dollars, everything. I would have preferred stealing from a richer man, but richer men do not stay at hotels like the Maxfield, not for more than a couple of hours. Still, it bothered me.

His name, according to the driver's license and the NMU card, was Edward Boleslaw. Mine is Alexander Penn. No doubt his friends call him Ed, or Eddie. My friends, when I had friends, called me Alex.

He was born in 1914, the year of Sarajevo, the year of the start of a war. I was born in 1929, the year of the crash.

Now I was wearing his clothes, and carrying five out of seven of his dollars.

There was no time. He would not bathe forever, he would eventually towel himself dry and pad across the room in his terrycloth robe and discover that he had been robbed. By then I had best be gone.

I opened the door. I looked at the dead whore again, and this time a sudden unexpected wave of revulsion went through me. I was unprepared for the reaction. It nearly knocked me off my feet. I got hold of myself, left the room, locked the door (they would open it, they would find her, locking the door would not change this) and walked down the hallway toward a red exit sign. I walked down three drab flights of stairs to the ground floor. The clock over the desk said that it was ten-thirty, and a sign next to the clock announced that checkout time was eleven o'clock.

The desk clerk, a light-skinned Negro with horn-rimmed glasses and a thin neat moustache, asked me if I would be staying another night. I shook my head. He asked for the key. I flipped it onto the desk.

I wondered whether I had used my own name when I signed in. It did not matter, my fingerprints would be all over the room anyway. I started for the door, expecting the desk clerk to call after me, expecting to be met at the door by police. He did not call. No police awaited me. I stepped outside into overly bright sunlight that hurt my eyes. I wanted a cigarette, I wanted a drink, I didn't know where to go.

HOTEL MAXFIELD, 324 WEST 49TH STREET, NEW YORK CITY. DROP IN ANY MAILBOX. WE PAY POSTAGE. That would be between Eighth and Ninth Avenues, on the downtown side of the street. I turned to my right and walked half a block to Eighth Avenue. I crossed Forty-ninth Street and walked a block north, and on the corner of Fiftieth and Eighth I found a drugstore. I went inside and broke Edward Boleslaw's five-dollar bill to buy a pack of cigarettes. I would need a razor, too, and blades, but I did not buy them now. I only had five dollars—$4.56 now, after buying the cigarettes, and the money would have to feed me and clothe me and shelter me until—

Until I gave up and called the police.

No. No, I would not call the police, I would not give myself up, I would not go back inside again.

No.

I lit a cigarette. I drew smoke into my lungs, and my head throbbed, and my hands shook. I went back to the counter and bought a tin of aspirin and took three tablets without water. It was difficult getting them down but I managed it. I put the aspirins in a pocket of Edward Boleslaw's trousers and put the cigarettes and matches in a pocket of Edward Boleslaw's shirt and left the drugstore and stood in the sunlight.

I did not know where to go.

· 3 ·

HOME IS WHERE, WHEN YOU HAVE TO GO THERE, THEY HAVE to take you in. That is the best definition of the word that I have ever heard. By its terms, I had no home. I had been born and raised in Chillicothe, Ohio, in which town my only living relative, a widowed aunt, still made her home. When I was sentenced to life imprisonment for the murder of Evangeline Grant, my Aunt Caroline had written me a brief note: *I hoped and prayed you would be hanged to spare you and all your family many years of shame. May you make your peace with God, and may He some day grant you rest.* By *all your family* she meant, I presume, herself.

I plotted a telephone conversation in my mind. "Aunt Caroline? This is Alex. You may have heard that I've been released. Yes, several months ago. No, I haven't gone back to teaching. No, nothing like that. But the reason I called, you see, is that I've gone and done it again. Gone and killed another girl; yes. Cut her throat, just like the last one. And why I'm calling, you see, is that this time I'm not going to give myself up to the police. Not this time. Instead I figured on coming out to Chillicothe and staying with you for a spell. Just while I pull myself together—"

Christ.

Before the murder—the first murder, the Evangeline Grant murder—I had had a wife. She was very good throughout the ordeal of arrest and trial. She stood by me through it all, Gwen did, and I have always felt that she quite forgave me for killing Evangeline Grant while never absolving me of my guilt for having had coitus with the girl. In any event she remained true-blue until I was safely inside, and visited me there twice, and divorced me in Alabama, moved to the West Coast, met someone in Los Angeles, and married him. I did not recall her married name, although I must have learned it at one time or another.

Hers was another doorstep on which I could not turn up. There were also the doorsteps of friends, though few remained, and few of those in New York. I had called a handful of men since I left prison. I had seen one of them, Doug MacEwan, and him only two or three times. And I had been only a little more successful at making new friends than at keeping the old. While I had made no enemies in prison, neither had I formed any firm relationships. Once I saw a fellow prisoner on the street and we passed one another without speaking. Another time Turk Williams looked me up. He offered me a job, not, I don't think, because he felt my talents were particularly adaptable to the wholesale heroin business but out of some impulse of gratitude. My own legal actions had opened the door to his cell, and I had further helped him prepare his appeal.

I did not take the job, no doubt to his relief. Nor did I see him again after that. He lived somewhere in Harlem and had left his phone number at my place on Ninth Street. It was probably still somewhere around the apartment.

Ah, yes. The apartment. For home, to use a more mundane definition, is also where you hang your hat, and I hung mine, and had for about ten weeks, on East Ninth Street between Avenues B and C, in a part of New York which is called the Lower East Side by traditionalists and the East Village by romantics.

I decided to go there now. Not because any urgent business called me there, but because now was probably the last chance I would have. At any moment now the desk clerk would bang on the door of my room at the Hotel Maxfield, announcing that it was time for me to depart. Then he would notice that I had already checked out, and so he would get the key and unlock the room, or else a chambermaid would perform that task. Whoever did the job, the body of the girl would be discovered, and within a half hour or so the police would arrive, and in a matter of hours after that my finger-prints would be identified (or faster identification would be accomplished from something left in my clothes, or, quite possibly, I would have used my real name in signing for the room), and before very long, perhaps that very afternoon, perhaps not until the following morning, the police would be knocking on the door of my apartment.

It would not do to be there when they arrived. And, certainly, there were reasons why I would want to get to the apartment. I had clothes there, clothes which fit me better than the borrowed clothing of Edward Boleslaw. There was no money—everything had been in my wallet, and my wallet was gone. There was a checkbook, though, that would do me little good; there was no place I knew of where I could cash a check, not on Sunday, and by the time the bank opened in the morning the police would know of me, and it would be dangerous to go to the bank. But clothing alone was incentive enough. I felt alarmingly conspicuous in his large shirt and flapping trousers, and horribly cramped in his small shoes.

I balanced time and money, which is like comparing apples and bananas, and took a taxi to my apartment. This, with tip, ate up two dollars of my $4.56. It seemed the lesser evil. There is simply no logical way to get that far east on Ninth Street by subway. Whatever combination of trains I might take, I would be left with a long walk. My feet couldn't take it, not in those shoes, nor could I afford the time. I took a taxi, and sat in back watching the meter, smoking my cigarettes, suffering from my headache, and struggling neither to think nor to plan nor to remember.

Of course I didn't have my key. I had to rouse the building superintendent, and together we climbed three joyless flights of stairs, he grumbling and I apologetic, and he opened the door for me and suggested that I take my key along with me next time. I forebore telling him that I had no key to take with me, or that I would never be returning to the apartment. He went away, and I removed Edward Boleslaw's clothing and showered (*Here's the smell of the blood still! All the perfumes of Arabia . . .*) and dressed anew in clothing of my own. Good presentable clothing: a gray sharkskin suit, a white shirt, black shoes, an unmemorable striped tie. Before dressing, but after showering (it's difficult to keep one's chronology straight) I shaved and combed my hair. Throughout all of this I was much more relaxed than I had expected to be. My hand did not shake while I shaved, and I did not even nick myself, a feat I usually perform even when unrattled by either hangover or guilt. I was quite calm right up to the point where I looked at myself in my mirror, all neatly dressed and neatly groomed and, if not handsome, not entirely badlooking either, and cocked a grin at myself, and tried a wink, and then, without warning, crumbled completely.

I think I wept. I don't know. There was a blank moment, and then I was sitting on my own narrow bed with my head in my hands and my eyes focused on the floor between my own feet.

One remembers odd things at odd moments. I remembered the last meeting with Morton J. Pillion, the warden of the prison in which I spent four years. He was a frail, birdlike man, gray of hair and pink of face, and from the first time I had met him I had felt he was altogether miscast for his role. A prison warden should be more like Broderick Crawford, and he was rather on the lines of an elderly Wally Cox.

He said, "You know, Alex, I'll miss you. Now don't feel you have to return the compliment. I suspect you're anxious to be outside."

"I don't know," I said.

"You don't even have to sit still for this talk, you know," he went on. "You're to be discharged at once. That's the language of the order. Not like a prisoner who's served his time and has to have that final interview with the Old Man whether he likes it or not. Improper representation by counsel, improper use of confession, oh, all of that. A free man. Care to walk out on me, Alex?"

"No."

"How do you feel?"

"I'm not sure."

"Understandable." He gave me a cigarette and a light. "The usual lecture contains a lot of tripe about the prisoner's having paid his debt to society. I don't like the phrase, but it's a convenient one. But you haven't paid your debt, have you, Alex? You committed a murder and now we're letting you out." He sighed, shook his head. "Know what you'll be doing now?"

"I'll look for work. I'm not sure what kind."

"You're a professor, of course—"

"I'm afraid that's out."

"Perhaps, though time does heal wounds. Even of this sort. What else are you qualified for?"

"Library work?"

"You've certainly done a fine job here. I'd gladly give you a reference. But you may have difficulty getting hired. How are you fixed financially?"

"I have some money saved. A savings account."

"Much?"

"Enough for the time being. I'm not rich. I'll have to work sooner or later, and God knows at what."

"Try to get something on your own merits. Without changing your name, or hoping your identity doesn't catch up with you. Know what I mean? Because people always find things out sooner or later, and you're better off it you don't set yourself up for a fall."

We talked a good deal about this, about what sort of work

I might get, about what town I would settle in—I was going back to New York, because that was the place I knew best, and because it is the easiest town in which to lose oneself and remain nearly anonymous.

Eventually he said, "You've never remembered it, have you?"

"The murder, you mean? No. Never."

"I wonder if that's good."

"What do you mean?"

"I'm not sure myself, Alex. I wonder if a person's better off losing the memory of a crime. Forgive me an unpardonable liberty, but I have to say this. The important thing is that you not repeat the offense."

I said nothing.

"Every man has a devil in him," Pillion said. "With some the devil lives close to the surface, and alcohol or some other force can liberate him. This happened to you, with disastrous results. You must never lose sight of the fact that it could very possibly happen again."

"I won't let it."

"I hope not." He toyed with desktop objects—a pen, a pipe, an ashtray. "Two things to guard against. First, you don't remember the murder itself. Second, you're being released; you're being told in effect that you're legally innocent. These elements can combine to fool you, lead you to think that it never really happened in the first place. The tree falling when no human ear can hear it, eh? No murder, no guilt, no need to guard against a repeat performance. Eh?"

"I'm afraid you're getting a little metaphysical—"

"Perhaps. I'm not certain. What's the saying? 'He who fails to learn from the past is condemned to repeat it.' I'm afraid I've gotten the words wrong, but you know my meaning, you're a historian yourself."

"Yes."

He lowered his eyes. "Actually, you're a lucky man. A very lucky man. You're getting a second chance, not because of anything you've done but because of a combination of circumstances. I hope you'll keep that devil buried. Or see a psychiatrist and exorcise him entirely. And I hope you'll stay far away from liquor. Some men can drink and some can't, and—"

"I always thought I was one who could."

"Perhaps you could have, at one time. Don't experiment. Stay away from drink. Keep the lid on tight. Learn from the past, Alex. God, yes, learn from the past, don't repeat it. It's not a good past. Don't repeat it."

I wanted to call him. I wanted to get him on the phone—better, to see him in person, in his office, sitting across the desk from him, telling him about it. I had not learned from the past, I had repeated it, and there would be no third chance.

I took some aspirin, then wandered around the apartment trying to think what it held that I might want to take with me. Certainly there must have been specific articles which might have been of value to a criminal on the run, but this was a role I had never before played and one to which I was consequently quite unaccustomed. I had to run. Presumably I had to run *somewhere*. But where? Embezzlers went to Brazil. Western gunmen went to the Badlands. Where did modern-day murderers go? And how?

Or did one merely attempt to avoid capture, staying in the same city, lurking in familiar haunts? That seemed unlikely. From what I had read, criminals usually headed for bright lights, the busy downtown sections of major cities. And there they were quickly caught. Or else they raced for the Mexican border, and were captured attempting to cross it.

Perhaps if I just went somewhere in the Midwest. But my face would be broadcast everywhere, newspapers, television. I would be recognized, I would be caught—

I left the apartment without taking anything with me. Not even my checkbook, nothing, nothing at all. I left the apartment and started walking.

· 4 ·

My FELLOW CONVICTS AND I WERE GREAT TELEVISION FANS. We liked most shows (except for the cute situation comedies, which almost everyone hated) but the crime programs were our favorite hands down. We loved *The Fugitive*. I've read thoughtful analyses of the show which suggest that it represents wish-fulfillment for the American public—Kimble is innocent, but he has to stay on the run, and thus has an excuse to lead an escapist life with no permanent ties, etc., etc., etc. It certainly represented wish-fulfillment for all of us. Because the cops were after the sonofabitch, but he was on the outside, and he stayed on the outside, and in the course of staying on the outside he ran across a statistically improbable quantity of goodlooking women.

For several years I never missed that program. In the summer I watched the re-runs. So you would have thought that I would have learned something about the problem of functioning as a fugitive from justice. It seemed now that all those weeks of watching David Janssen scamper from hither to yon had done me no good at all. He always went interesting places and did interesting things. He got jobs, colorful jobs, and he concealed his true identity with the resourcefulness of Clark Kent, and he always knew which people to take into his confidence. But, more than that, he always seemed to be guided by some special sort of master plan. He never sat around like a dolt wondering what to do next, or where to go, or whether it wouldn't be better to drown himself. When all else failed, he could start hunting the one-armed man again. But in the meantime there was always a place for him to go, a bit of business for him to involve himself in, a new road for him to follow.

I was an utter failure as a fugitive. I walked uptown to Fourteenth Street and west to Union Square. I ate baked beans and scrambled eggs and home fries at the Automat, and drank a few cups of coffee. I took a subway to Times Square. I got off the subway with seventy-five cents left. I spent fifty-five cents to get into a Forty-second Street movie, a pair of westerns, Audie Murphy, Randolph Scott. I spent ten cents on a candy bar. I sat in the balcony and smoked cigarettes and watched the movies. I had ten cents left, and I intended to spend it on a second candy bar as soon as I was hungry again. I was a complete failure as a fugitive and it barely bothered me.

While Audie Murphy and Randolph Scott led the forces of good to their inevitable triumph over the forces of evil, I hunched in my seat and followed the action on the screen, letting the films bake my psyche as a Turkish bath might have done for my body. Everything drained out. The headache went away, the fear, the pain, everything. Anesthesia.

And the hours slipped neatly away. If I were going to escape from New York City now was emphatically the time to do it. In a matter of hours the police would be looking for me, and once that happened bus terminals and airports and railway stations would cease to be safe. (It occurred to me now that I should have taken my checkbook, that the airlines would have accepted a check. It had not occurred to me before. And it no longer seemed to matter. I was watching the movie, I would go on watching the movie; as long as I stayed where I was nothing bad could happen to me. The cocoon mentality.)

When I entered the theater, the Audie Murphy picture was

about a third gone. I watched it to the end, and then I
watched the Randolph Scott picture, and then I watched a
coming attraction for something and a Roadrunner cartoon
and a two-minute advertisement for the goodies available at
the downstairs refreshment stand in the main lobby. Then I
watched the Audie Murphy picture to the point where I came
in, and, since there was no particular place to go next, I
stayed there to watch it through to the end again.

Remember, said an inner voice.

No. No, I'd rather not.

Remember last night.

No. I had a blackout. I'm entitled to a blackout.

Lift the curtain. Bring back bits and pieces of it—

Why?

*He who fails to learn from the past is condemned to repeat
it.*

But it had already been repeated. Why remember it again?
Look, there's Audie Murphy, here's the part where he beats
the hell out of the rotten crooked sheriff, watch it now—

Remember.

I gave up and sat back and closed my eyes and turned off
the movie and let myself remember.

It had, tritely, been a day like any other day. Outside, as
inside, I had come to learn the safety and security of pattern,
of habit. I had learned not to rush things but to let them
come as they would, living my own life in a neat and orderly
fashion that would supply a counterfeit purpose when none in
fact existed. I lived frugally, in my two ill-furnished rooms on
East Ninth Street. I ate out of cans or took meals at a cafete-
ria around the corner. I shaved each morning, and I wore
clean clothing every day, and I made myself busy although I
had nothing to be busy about. I walked to Tompkins Square
Park and played chess with some of the elderly pensioners who
sunned themselves there. I wandered to the public library and
read all manner of books and magazines. Frequently, but not

invariably, I bought the *Times* and read the classified ads, neatly marking those offering jobs for which I was presumably qualified.

In the beginning I had actually answered some of those ads, but I learned quickly that this was a futile occupation. For the time being I had several thousand dollars of savings set aside, and the way I was living it would last quite awhile. When it ran out I would find a way to avoid starvation, some sort of day labor job, something anonymous.

There had been one job offer, Turk's suggestion that I might help him cut heroin with sugar and quinine and package it for sale to his various outlets. "You want to make it on the outside," he argued, "you got to get something sweet going. A cat like you or me, once he been inside, ain't nobody going to make him president of U.S. Steel. You need to find a hustle."

And Doug MacEwan's suggestion, while geared more along socially acceptable lines, made much the same point. He thought I ought to go into business for myself, as small businessmen do not need to provide backgrounds and references for an employer's satisfaction. I had almost as much difficulty seeing myself as the proprietor of a candy store as I did picturing myself in business with Turk. The best I could do was consider a mail-order business, something that would at least keep me away from my fellow man, and now and then I'd muddle through a library book on mail-order techniques. But as long as I had money, you see, I daydreamed of teaching again, and as long as the dream remained even vaguely alive, however impossible I might realize it to be, I could not take any other sort of career too seriously. When the money ran out it would be a different matter.

But I digress. What I remembered, sitting in the balcony, what I willed myself to remember, was not the course of the average day, the course of several months worth of days, but the course of one particular day.

I awoke. I showered, I shaved, I dressed. I breakfasted in

my apartment, a glass of reconstituted orange juice, a cup of instant coffee, two slices of toast—

Details. Immaterial, forget them.

After breakfast I left the apartment. I was dressed then in the same clothes I had later found, blood-covered, in room 402 at the Hotel Maxfield. I went—where? To the library? To the park?

No. No, I went up to Times Square. It was a good day, a beautiful not too hot and not too cold day, the air clearer than New York air usually is, and I walked to Times Square. It was a very long walk, and I covered the distance slowly. And I had slept late that morning. I must have reached Times Square around noon, perhaps a bit past noon.

And then what?

I certainly hadn't begun drinking right away. Why couldn't I remember it all? What was wrong?

Ah, yes.

I had wandered Forty-second Street—the shooting gallery, the Fascination parlor, the bookstores, the cafeterias, the whole tawdry stretch of the street from Broadway to Eighth Avenue and back again. I remembered it now as an aimless, pointless ramble. And yet, had I been sufficiently introspective at the time, I would have recognized the point of it all. For I was no stranger to Forty-second Street. It had always been the starting point of my rambles, the embarkation point for bouts of drinking and whoring in those dim days before I murdered Evangeline Grant.

In a bookstore, a brightly lit bookstore stocked with nudist magazines and paperbound novels entitled *Sin Shack* and *Trailer Trollop* and *Campus Tramp*, and pamphlets entitled *Confessions of a Spanker* and *Sweet Bondage* and *The Strange Sisterhood of Madame Adista*, I leafed through a bin of photographs of more or less nude girls. I glanced laconically at this picture and that picture and this picture and that picture, without any real interest, with no response, and then I looked at one picture and God alone knows how it differed in my eyes from the rest, but quite without warning a stab of painful desire seared my groin, and I reeled away from the bin of pictures as if gored in the vitals by a mad bull.

I had not made love to a woman since Evangeline Grant, whom, as you may recall, I subsequently killed. I had not made love to a woman in over four years, in nearly four and one-half years, and I honestly thought I had lost all desire. I had since seen many pictures of girls, both clothed and nude. I had looked at them with admiration, with enthusiasm, but never with lust. I had grown to feel that this was no longer a part of my life, that I had killed it when I killed Evangeline Grant.

And now one picture among many, a photograph which I would now be quite incapable of distinguishing from its bin-mates, had proved me wrong.

Yes. I remembered it now. Reeling out of there, stunned, honestly stunned, embarrassed beyond belief by the insistent and undeniable physical manifestation of this reaction, walking hunched oddly forward in ineffectual camouflage, certain that everyone was staring at me, scampering foolishly out of the dreary little shop. And automatically blindly stupidly following my erection down the street and around the corner to the nearest bar, where I promptly proved and discovered beyond any shadow of a doubt that I had not lost my taste for liquor, either.

I remembered the bar. It was one of those no-nonsense places where the price of every drink is posted on massive cardboard signs over the bar, with triple shots offered at special bargain rates. A drinking man's bar, with no frills or unnecessary embellishments. "Its not fancy but it's good." An alcoholic's Horn & Hardart.

I remembered taking out my wallet and extracting a dollar bill, and looking at it, and putting it back, and taking out instead a ten-dollar bill and putting that on top of the bar. Proof that I knew, before the first drink, that I would be having a good deal more drinks than a single dollar would pay for.

I had not had a woman in over four years. I had not had a drink in over four years. I had the drink—I could even remember the brand, a cheap blended whiskey. I tossed it down, and coughed, and set the shot glass on top of the bar and motioned for a refill. I remembered all of that. I remembered it vividly.

The Audie Murphy picture ended without my paying any attention to it. I lit a cigarette. The Randolph Scott picture started again. I looked at the clock a few yards to the left of the screen, blue hands, blue numerals. It was almost five o'clock. By now they knew. By now the alarm was probably out, and in a few hours the early editions of the *Times* and the *Daily News* would hit the streets with my picture there for all to see. I might already be on the radio newscasts. I would almost certainly make the eleven o'clock television news.

I stayed where I was. For a while I watched the movie, and it was utterly unfamiliar to me, as if I had not already seen it from start to finish once that day. Neither the visual images nor the dialogue seemed even remotely familiar. How curious the mind is.

No one knows very much about blackouts, the how and why of them, all of that. Some heavy drinkers never have them. Some heavy drinkers always have them. And the great run of drinkers have tiny stretches of blankness; they lose the last half hour or so before bedtime, or have little hazy spots for the periods of intense drunkenness.

Often you can recapture bits of the memory that has been lost. You rarely get the whole thing, but you can dredge up bits and pieces, scraps and shreds. One memory is a clue, a handle to another chunk of memory, and while the jigsaw puzzle is never quite complete, a man can often put together enough of the pieces to get a good idea of the over-all design.

It was thus with Evangeline Grant. I remembered picking

her up. I did not remember taking her to the hotel—one rather like the Maxfield, and no more than three blocks away. I remembered entering the room with her. I remembered her body moving under mine, and I remember to this day, and without any particular sense of lust, all the details of her body. I remember the feel of her flesh in a way that transcends normal memory, and I have wondered whether it is not false memory indeed, for it strikes me as incredible that I can remember this once-possessed whore's flesh, taken in deep drunkenness, a flash of memory in a sea of black, that I can remember this flesh in a far more vivid fashion than I can recall, for example, the oft-possessed body of my own wife.

That I remember. I don't remember the murder, a knife slash across the jugular, blood spurting, everything. I remember none of it.

Well.

The point of this is, simply, that a blackout is a selective thing, and yet there would appear to be something of random chance in its operation. I can for example recall evenings, pleasant social evenings, pleasant evenings of social drinking and conversation with faculty members and their wives, pleasant social evenings after which I would awaken with a three-hour memory lapse and the horrid certainty that I had in that unremembered gap done something unpardonable, committed some irredeemable sin, insulted some dear friend, performed, in short, some nameless but unspeakable horror. And I would subsequently find out that I had done nothing wrong at all, that I had impressed my friends as having been completely sober, at least no more than slightly high.

And yet it would be blacked out, gone.

Well.

Now, while Randolph Scott shot Comanches, I sucked on a cigarette and picked at my brain like a fussy eater. From the first drink there was no neat chronology, no full history. There were only flashes of memory, some vivid, some fuzzy, some barely present at all. I played with the memories like an archaeologist with a shredded scroll of papyrus, trying to straighten them out and fit them in place and read meaning into them.

A boisterous conversation with a large red-haired man, a merchant seaman. Each of us standing rounds of drinks, and then something that he said (his words lost to memory now) and I threw a punch at him. I missed, and fell on the floor, and I think he kicked me. Then several men hustled me out of the bar and dropped me at the curb. They were neither rough nor gentle, they took me out as if carrying garbage, took me out, dropped me.

Trying to get into a sidewalk phone booth, but it was occupied, a woman, a fat woman with an armload of packages making a phone call in the booth, and I outside, trying to get in, and stumbling from booth to curb and being violently ill in the gutter. Late at night by then, streetlights, neon, and I puked up my guts at the curb while the world cautiously ignored me.

Later or earlier, a cop trying to decide whether or not to run me in. Was I sick? Was I all right? Could I get home myself? God, if only he had run me in. God in heaven, if only he had run me in.

But when had I got hold of the knife? Where and when had I picked up the girl?

The girl's face then, remembered vividly, not as I had seen it that morning in death but as I had seen it the night before on Seventh Avenue somewhere between Forty-sixth Street and Fiftieth Street. The girl's face, very pale skin, black hair worn long and loose, a thin sharp nose, a red mouth, intensely blue eyes, and the waxen sunken eyelids of a heroin addict. The slightly junked-up stare of those immaculate blue eyes. A slender girl, a reed of a girl. No makeup, just the lipstick. Low-heeled shoes. Toothpick legs. A black skirt, a wet blouse. Breasts full beneath the blouse, large breasts for so slim a girl. Age? She was as old and as young as a whore.

Her name was Robin. I remember now, her name was

Robin. At least that was what she told me, and I told her my name was Alex.

An echo—

"Hi, honey."

"Well, hello."

"Do you want to go out?" I still remembered the euphemisms. Four years, four and a half years, I still remembered the euphemisms. Some things you never forget, like swimming.

"Sure." An arm tucked in mine. "How much can you give me?"

"Ten?"

"Could you give me twenty?"

"I guess."

"You're not too drunk, are you, honey?"

"I'm all right."

"Cause it's no good if you're too drunk, and all."

"I'm all right."

"You got a room?"

"No."

"Well, I know a hotel—"

Then a long blank stretch. Nothing, no matter how I go over it. Just nothing. Evidently we walked or rode to the hotel. I've no idea which. We could have taken a cab, we could have walked. Perhaps the newspapers will tell me what happened, perhaps someone will have seen us walking together, perhaps a cab driver will remember conveying us to the Maxfield. But I cannot summon up the memory.

Oh. I used my name at the hotel. My own name, my own address. Just the single lie of *Mr. & Mrs.*, the usual hotel room lie. But my own name.

That would make it easier for the police, as if it were not already sufficiently easy for them.

Memory of checking in, no memory of getting to the room. Just the memory of being in the room, and giving her money, and getting undressed. And Robin getting undressed.

This last memory was too vivid, too sharp. I cowered in my balcony seat and closed my eyes to shut out Randolph Scott. The white blouse, the black skirt, both off. The breasts—I had not previously believed them—bobbing in a white bra. "Help me with this, honey?" And turning her back to me so that I could unhook that bra. The silken feeling, so long forgotten, of her sweet skin. My hands surrounding her, cupping those breasts, those unbelieved breasts.

(The memory ached. Pain in the groin, in the pit of the stomach. A fantastic visual and tactile memory, total recall of how she looked and felt. Those thin wrists, those thin legs, that round bottom, flat tummy, soft, soft, oh!)

I could not cease touching her. I had to touch and embrace all of her, every square inch of her.

"Oh, lie down, honey. Here, let me French it for you—"

Floating, on a bed, on a cloud, on the waves. Boneless, limp, floating. The memory of those hands, of that mouth. The Hindu flutist charming the snake. Robin Red Breast, Robin Hood. Sweet Robin. Here, let me French it for you.

Four and a half years.

Some things once learned are never forgotten, like swimming.

There the memory ended. I fought with it, played with it, and for a long time I could dredge up no more of it. I wanted to remember the killing, and yet I did not want to, and I fought a quiet battle with myself, then gave up at last and went downstairs to the stand in the lobby. I spent my last dime on a candy bar and took it upstairs again. I found the same seat, unwrapped the candy bar, ate it in small thoughtful bites, and watched the movie for a few minutes.

Then more memory.

We had finished, Robin and I. I lay, eyes closed, sated, fulfilled. A door opened—Robin leaving? What? A variety of sounds which I did not open my eyes to investigate.

Then—

I could almost get it, but at first I was afraid. I sat in my seat and clenched my eyes tightly shut and made small hard fists of both my hands. I fought and won, and it came into focus.

A hand clasped over Robin's mouth *but not my hand* and another hand holding a knife *but not my hand* and Robin struggling in someone's arms *but not my arms* and a knife slashing slashing *but not my knife* and blood everywhere but I could not move, I could not move, I could only gasp and moan and, at last, slip back under blackness.

I sat bolt upright in my seat. Sweat poured from my forehead. My heart was pounding and I could not breathe.

I remembered.

I hadn't killed her. I hadn't done it. Somebody else killed her. Somebody else did it, wielded the knife, cut the ivory throat, killed, murdered.

I remembered!

· 5 ·

IT WAS DARK WHEN I LEFT THE MOVIE THEATER. FORTY-SECOND Street sparkled with the wilted glitter of a Christmas tree on Twelfth Night. Pairs of policemen and pairs of homosexuals cruised blindly by one another. I kept my face turned toward the store windows and walked toward Eighth Avenue with my head lowered. I held my breath for the last fifty yards and let it out in a rush as I turned the corner.

I absolutely had to have money. The last dime, gone to buy a candy bar, could have bought me a phone call instead. If I could reach MacEwan, I could borrow money. Without money I had no chance at all. No chance to stay away from the police, no chance to find out whose hand had wielded the knife that slashed Robin's throat.

I was disgusted at the alacrity with which I had divested myself of Edward Boleslaw's five dollars. Taxi, cigarettes, food, subway, movies, candy. Gone.

Yet it was not difficult to understand how I had permitted this to happen. Until the last fragment of memory returned in that theater balcony, until the sudden incredible revelation that I was not guilty, that I had not killed little Robin, the idea of making a genuine attempt to remain free was basically unreal. I had been taking no positive steps to avoid the law. On the contrary, I had merely failed to surrender myself. By impoverishing myself once again, I did no more than advance the inevitable moment of capture or surrender.

Now, with the last dime spent, I had a reason to remain a fugitive. Once arrested, I was finished. I had provided the police with a perfectly sound case against me. No assistant district attorney could be so unpolished as to lose such a case, no jury so blind as to fail to convict.

I knew, with absolute certainty, that I was innocent. And there was no reason on earth for anyone else on earth to believe me.

A man, very tall, with long hair neatly combed, dressed in an Italian silk suit and wearing black shoes with sharply pointed toes, emerged from a rooming house on Eighth Avenue a few doors south of Forty-first Street. He turned my way, and I moved from the shadows to meet him, and hoped as I did so that my face was not one he had recently seen on television.

I said, "I hope you'll pardon me, I hate to impose, but my wallet was lifted on Times Square. I didn't even realize it was gone until I got to the subway toll booth. If you could spare twenty cents—"

Liquid brown eyes met mine. They showed sympathy with just the smallest touch of humor beneath.

"Of course," he said. "A dreadful lot, these pickpockets. The city's absolutely turned jungle, hasn't it?"

"Yes."

"Will a token help you?"

"Yes, it will. Sorry to bother you this way—"

"Don't happen to have the time, do you?"

I looked at my empty wrist, then at him. "Don't have my watch," I said. "Must have left it home."

"Got your watch too, did he?"

"No, I must have—"

He ran a long-fingered hand through his wavy hair. "Oh, I sympathize," he said, smiling gently. "These boys are dangerous, there's no gainsaying that. We know better than to go with them, don't we? They rob us with impunity. We can hardly scream for the police, after all." A languid sigh. "And yet go with them we do. For they are such a delight at times, are they not?"

"Uh."

"I'm for uptown, if you'd care to share a taxi—"

"I live in Brooklyn."

"Ah. Ships that pass in the night." He handed me a subway token. "I hope you didn't lose very much money?"

"Not too much."

"You're fortunate." A quick smile. "Better luck next time, friend."

People were queued up at the token booth. I waited until the line was gone, then went to the booth and slid the token through the window. "Better cash this in," I said. "Won't do me any good in Spokane."

The attendant took the token, poked two dimes my way. I went upstairs and outside. I walked half a dozen blocks down Eighth Avenue looking for an outdoor telephone booth, then gave up and called from a cigar store.

Doug answered.

I said, "It's Alex. I have to tell you—"

"Oh, God," he said. "Where have they got you? I'll get a lawyer down to see you. I—"

"I'm not in custody."

"You haven't turned yourself in yet? You'd better. The police were here a few hours ago, asking about you. And they showed a photo of you on television. It'll be in the morning papers. My God, Alex, what happened?"

"Nothing happened." We were both silent for a moment, and then I said, "I didn't kill the girl, Doug."

"Oh?"

"I was with her, but that's no crime. Someone else killed her."

"Who?"

"I don't know."

"Then how do you—"

"I *saw* someone else kill her. It's the last thing I remember. I can't remember what he looked like. Just a hand with a knife in it."

"You were drinking."

"Yes."

"Memory's a funny thing, Alex. Of course the police can try to help you. Pentothal, drugs like that, they might improve your memory. Fill things out."

"I can't go to the police."

"I don't see what else you *can* do—"

"I can't go to them."

"Why not?"

It was a thoroughly maddening conversation. "Because they won't for a minute believe me," I said, "any more than you do."

The sentence echoed back and forth over the telephone line. Neither of us had anything in particular to append to it. Finally, his voice somewhat different now, he said, "Why are you calling me?"

"I need money."

"To make a run for it? You'll never do it."

"Not to run, damn it. To survive while I find out who in hell killed the girl. Doug, please, humor me. *Pretend* to believe me."

"Oh, Christ—"

"Let me have a couple of hundred in cash. You'll get it back."

"Are you that flat?"

"Well, I can't exactly run around cashing checks. Can I come up there? I've got ten cents in my pocket, that's all. I'll find a way to get another dime for the subway. All right?"

"I don't want you coming up here."

"Why not?"

"The police were here, don't you understand? I don't want to be an accessory—"

I stopped listening. I tuned in again long enough to hear something to the effect that, after all, this was not the first time this had happened, and then I tuned out again and gave up.

"Alex? Are you still there?"

"Yes."

"Tell me where you are. I'll come down, give you the dough. But I don't want you coming up here. Fair enough?"

Tell me where you are. I almost did, but the operator cut in just then, requesting that I deposit another five cents. I'd already wasted ten cents on the call, and that was enough. I stalled her.

Tell me where you are. And he, my good friend, acting no doubt in my own best interests, would tell the police where to find me.

"Broadway and Eighty-sixth Street," I said. "Southwest corner." And hung up.

· 6 ·

I WALKED DOWNTOWN. I HAD ONE DIME LEFT, AND WOULD HAVE
needed another to take the subway, and it did not seem worth
the effort to hunt up and hustle a second sympathetic faggot.
It was simpler to walk.

I stayed on Eighth Avenue as far as Thirty-third Street.
Further down there were a batch of Greek and Arabic night-
clubs, belly dancers and such, and more street and sidewalk
traffic than I cared to be exposed to. At Thirty-third I cut over
to Seventh, and stayed on Seventh down to the Village. The
Village, too, was crowded, but there was no help for that.

At first, as I walked, I thought about money. It was my
most immediate need. I was neither hungry nor tired just yet,
but I could anticipate being both before very long; I would
need food and a safe place to sleep, and money could secure
them both. I considered letting a homosexual pick me up and
then rolling him. The tall slender man who had given me the
token had suggested that much to me by assuming I had met
just such a fate myself. He did make it sound the simplest of
crimes to carry off, but I couldn't see myself in the role. It
would be embarrassing, before and during and after. No.

But there was another way, one which would permit me to
draw from my own experience. And, in a sense, even an old
score. I thought about it and worked out as many details as it
seemed profitable to work out in advance. I got it all set in
my mind and then stopped thinking about it.

And thought instead of Robin.

Facts: I had not killed her. Someone else had killed her. Someone had killed her in such a way as to leave me the obvious villain, obvious even to myself. Someone had wanted me saddled with her murder.

Facts: I had not merely been a convenience for the killer. He had gone to great lengths to make sure I was caught. Soaked my clothes with blood. Stole my watch and wallet to make escape all the more difficult. Fitted all the trappings of the murder scene to the earlier murder of Evangeline Grant. The slashed throat, the passed-out post-coital killer, everything.

Conclusion: The murder of Robin had been the means to an end. She had been killed solely to frame me. I drank, I blacked out, I stumbled around, I picked up Robin, and all the while the killer lurked in shadows, following, waiting. Robin had bad luck, but I had an enemy.

Who, for the love of God?

I lit my last cigarette. The question was absurd. I didn't even *know* anyone. I stayed in my apartment, I played chess, I read, I thought about applying for jobs I could never get. I carried on no love affairs, threatened no one's career, and generally interacted with virtually no one. That there was any person in my life with any motive whatsoever for framing me for murder was utterly inconceivable. Barring the existence of a maniacally impractical joker, it was quite impossible that anyone could have done this to me on purpose.

Odd that I didn't make the obvious connection then. But I was fatigued, after all, and sufficiently dizzy with the knowledge that I was innocent of Robin's murder. And the mind tends to take for granted whatever it has learned to acknowledge as fact. So, however obvious the next bit of reasoning might later seem, I missed it for the time being.

A partial explanation may lie in the coincidence of my reaching Fourteenth Street at just that point in my train of thought. I crossed the street and moved through the northern edge of Greenwich Village, and at once my mind busied itself with thoughts of money and how it was to be obtained.

I knew I'd find the sailors. It was just a question of time. There are always several groups of sailors in the Village, and they always drink, and they always look for girls, and it never works out right for them. They all come from places like Des Moines and Topeka and Chillicothe, and they have all heard wondrous stories about Greenwich Village, where all the men are queer and all the women believe in Free Love—a situation which, were it true, would have to engender extraordinary frustration all around.

Poor sailors. There are no streetwalkers in the Village. There are any number of lovely young ladies, of all ages and colors and temperaments, and most of these young ladies look promiscuous, and many of them surely are, and none of them are interested in sailors. They all hate sailors. No one knows why; it seems to be traditional.

I met my sailors just as they were leaving a lesbian bar on Cornelia Street. There were three of them, and they were all somewhere between drinking age and voting age. They had evidently not known the place was a lesbian club. They had evidently not known that the girls therein had even less use for sailors than the average Village females. They had evidently made passes at some of the femmes and had been subsequently put down rather forcefully by some of the butches, and now they were trying to decide whether to be shocked or amused.

The saddest part was that they obviously felt that they were the first sailors to whom this sort of thing had ever happened, and for this reason they were both loathing and treasuring the moment. They were definitely not the first sailors to whom this sort of thing had ever happened. It always happens.

I fell in with them.

We walked and talked together. We talked of lesbians. We

talked of women and whiskey the world over. We talked, before very long, of the desirability of locating female companionship as soon as possible.

"I hear the mayor calls this town Fun City," said one of the sailors, the youngest and drunkest and loudest. "What do you figure is his idea of fun, the mayor's?"

"Maybe a fast game of parcheesi."

"The mayor," said the third, "has never been to Tokyo."

"Look here, Lou," said the first, "you *live* here, right? You must know where we can find some chickens."

Lou was my name, for the moment. Theirs were Red, Johnny, and Canada. Canada was the oldest, Red was the tallest, and Johnny was the youngest and drunkest and loudest. They took me to a bar and insisted on buying me a drink. I ordered milk, mumbling apologetically about an ulcer. I wanted a drink, and thought I could handle it without any trouble, but caution seemed indicated. They had a couple of rounds, flashed large rolls of bills, ogled some girls, and talked again about the need that was paramount in their minds. We left the bar, and they suggested once again that I might know some agreeable women.

"If I thought you boys were really serious—"

"You kidding, Lou?"

"Well, there are three girls I know who might be interested. Just kids, really. Nineteen or twenty. Let's see—Barbara's an actress, and I think Sheila and Jan are dancers, though they don't get much work. Beautiful girls, and they like to have a good time."

I let them coax details out of me. The three girls shared an apartment in the neighborhood. They weren't tramps or anything of the sort, but they would spend a night with a fellow who came well recommended; after all, they had to eat, and show business was hard on a beginner with no additional source of income. They only took guests for the whole night, and then they liked to make it a party, with plenty to drink and soft music on the record player and nonstop bedroom activity.

"Real wild Village women, huh?"

"So what are we waiting for? C'mon, Lou—be a buddy!"

Well, I explained, there were other considerations. Price, for example. The girls were no back-alley hookers. I wasn't sure of the price but I thought it was twenty or twenty-five dollars, and that might be more than the boys wanted to pay.

"That doesn't sound so bad, not for all night."

"Look, I'll level with you, Lou. This is our first night on shore in months. We're okay in the money department, know what I mean? Twenty or twenty-five is not about to break us."

And there was the question of the girls' availability. They might be out on dates, or they might have made prior arrangements, or—

"You can check it out, can't you?"

"I suppose I could call them—"

"Give 'em a call, Lou."

We stopped at another bar. The boys had a drink while I went to the phone booth in the back, dropped my dime, and dialed an incomplete number. I chatted to myself for a few minutes, put the phone on the hook, recovered my dime from the coin return slot, and rejoined the trio at the bar.

I said, "I think we better forget it."

"What's the matter? They busy?"

"No, but—"

"But what?"

Reluctantly, I let them get the story from me. The girls were at home, and available. But they were very worried about the possibility of getting arrested. A good friend of theirs, also an amateur and a part-time model, had been arrested by a plainclothesman just a week ago and this had made them very nervous. At the present time they were restricting their contacts to men they already knew.

"What it amounts to," I said, "is that they won't take money from a stranger. They'd have to get the cash in advance and then act as though the whole affair was a party, with no mention of money or anything. And they'd have to be sure that you guys aren't cops."

"Us? You got to be kidding."

I shrugged. "Listen, I trust you," I said. "But they never met you. You'd be surprised the way vice squad detectives dress up like sailors. Especially this time of the month, when they're in a hurry to get their quota of arrests. The girls are nervous. I talked to Barbara, and she said they'd rather go hungry than take a chance on getting arrested."

I had to lead them along. But they followed well enough, and they finally figured out the suggestion they were supposed to make. The girls knew me, they pointed out. So how would it be if they gave me the money and I went up to see the girls and make the arrangements? Then the girls could tuck the dough away somewhere and they would come to their apartment and it would be as if there was no money involved at all.

I thought it over and admitted that it might work out. "I'll call them again," I said. "It looked so hopeless at the time that I told them to forget it—"

"Jesus, Lou, I hope they didn't find somebody else since then."

"Well," I said, "I'll call them."

This time they clustered around the phone booth. I dialed a full seven-digit number at random and got a recording which assured me that the number I had dialed was not a working number. I talked with the recording, listened, talked, and finally hung up.

"Well?"

"A few problems," I admitted. "Since it's a Sunday, all the liquor stores are closed. They've got liquor on hand, but that pushes the price up. You may not want to go that high."

"How high?"

"A package deal—all three of you for an even hundred dollars."

They looked at each other. I read their faces, and evidently it was higher than they would have liked it, but not out of reach by any means. There was a second or two of silence, so I threw the clincher.

"It sounded high to me," I said. "I told Barbara I wanted ten per cent for setting things up, and she agreed. Believe, me, I don't want to make money this way, not on you fellows. Forget my ten, and I'll give her ninety dollars, that's thirty apiece. But don't tell her, understand? If the girls mention money, and the chances are they won't, but if they do, you gave me a hundred bucks. Understand?"

That did it. I was the greatest guy in the world, they assured me, and they wanted to buy me a drink again, but I reminded them of my ulcer. It was a shame there weren't four girls, they told me. Then I could join them. It was really a shame, because I was one great guy, the greatest, and they thought I was terriffic.

They gave me ninety dollars in tens. We left the bar, and the four of us walked over Greenwich Avenue to Tenth Street and down Tenth to Waverley Place. I picked the largest building on the block, told them to wait directly across the street, and that I would be down in ten minutes or less. They waited, and I crossed the street and went into the vestibule. I rang the bells for the four sixth-floor apartments, and at least two of them buzzed to admit me. I opened the door and went inside.

There was no back exit as far as I could see. That would have been the easiest way, and I had been trying to find a building with a back exit, but I couldn't remember one. This would have to do. I went on inside and climbed one flight of stairs, took off my shoe, put the money in it, and put the shoe back on. I waited an appropriate stretch of time and went back downstairs and opened the front door. I motioned to them, and they came across the street on the run.

"Apartment 6-B," I said. I was holding the door open so that we wouldn't have to play games with the buzzer. "Don't use the elevator. Take the stairs. Right up to the sixth floor and ring two short and one long. Got it?"

"Two short and one long."

"Right. It's all set, and the girls are waiting for you. Enjoy yourselves."

If no one was home at 6-B they might spend as much as an hour inside, convinced that I was on the up-and-up and the girls were cheating them. If somebody answered the door there would be an unfortunate scene, and eventually the boys would know just how they had been taken. Either way they had five flights of stairs to climb, and I did not intend to wait for their return.

They hurried inside, thanking me profusely, pounding up the stairs. I went outside and walked very speedily for three blocks. The stack of bills in my shoe had me limping oddly. Then a cab came along, and I stuck out a hand and caught it.

It was hard to believe how easy it had been. The words and gestures were all there when I needed them and the sailors never missed their cues. Now, in the cab, I was shaking. But while it was building I had been genuinely calm.

After all, the Murphy game is an exceptionally easy con to pull off. The sailors' drunken naivete hadn't hurt, but they could have been older and soberer and it wouldn't have helped them. Almost anyone will fall for it the first time around.

I lost thirty dollars like that once, years ago. And now had ninety back, which put me sixty dollars ahead of the game. Bread upon the waters—

· 7 ·

THE HOTEL WAS ON THIRTY-SEVENTH STREET BETWEEN PARK AND
Lexington. In the bathroom of Room 401 there was a mirror,
and in the mirror there was a face which looked altogether
too much like mine.

Still, there were differences. I still looked like me, but I no
longer looked like my description. My hair, normally a dark
brown, was now a rather washed-out-gray. I had had all of it;
now, with the aid of a razor, I had provided myself with
something of a receding hairline. An all-night drugstore had
furnished me with the necessary paraphernalia.

The face in the mirror was the face I would probably be
wearing in ten or fifteen years. If I lived that long.

I had not expected to be able to sleep. By the time I was
through with my work as an amateur makeup man, the city
was yawning outside my window, impatient for the day to
begin. I dropped into bed and closed my eyes and started to
think things out, and before I could begin to get my thoughts
organized I was under, and slept for ten hours without
stirring.

When I awoke finally I looked at myself in the mirror
again. I needed a shave and thought briefly of growing a
beard or moustache. This struck me as a bad idea—men with
beards or moustaches are more noticeable, and one automati-

cally wonders what they would look like without facial hair. I wanted as little attention paid to me as possible. I'd picked up a copy of the *News* before registering at the hotel, and I had studied the picture they ran under the headline GIRL KILLER DOES IT AGAIN! The photo was one they had taken upon my release from prison (at which time the headline read PLAYGIRL SLAYER FREE AGAIN) and it was not an especially good likeness to begin with. With the gray hair, with a bit of a slouch and a slower, more elderly walk, I ought to stand something of a chance.

I left the hotel, had eggs and sausages at a luncheonette around the corner. My hotel rent was paid a week in advance—I'd told them something about the airlines having done something unusual with my luggage. I forced myself to dawdle over a second cup of coffee, fighting the urge to rush back to the safety of the hotel room. After all, it would not be safe forever. I was better off using it not as a refuge but as a base of operations. It would not do to let the police find the murderer. I had to find him myself, and the longer I waited the more elusive he would no doubt become.

Who on earth was he?

Someone who hated me. Someone who wanted me well out of the way. Someone who would inherit my money or take my job or steal my wife once I had been deftly removed from the picture.

Except that I had no wife and no job and very little money. And no known enemies. And no friends who might be enemies in secret. And no women who might be women scorned. I was a threat to no one, an obstacle to no one, a confidant to no one, a lover to no one. I scarcely existed.

Years ago, of course, it had been different. I was an up-and-coming young professor with a book half-finished and an emerging reputation in academic circles. I had a wife, I had friends, I was a person. But now . . .

Then daylight dawned. I sat stunned for a full minute. I stood up at last, dropped some coins on the formica table, took my check to the cashier, paid, left. The afternoon sun hurt my eyes. I wondered if a pair of drugstore sunglasses might help my disguise, or if they would be more apt to direct attention my way. I decided that this was something I would think about later, when I did not have infinitely more important things to contemplate.

How had I missed it before? It was extraordinary. And yet when one's mind has been painfully, tortuously conditioned to accept something as fact, one is not quick to challenge that fact thereafter.

I walked. A policeman glanced my way, then returned to the job of directing traffic. I shivered at his glance. I lowered my head, concentrated on my walk, my shoulders stooped, my head bowed, my feet covering the ground more slowly than usual. I walked to my hotel, and I walked past my hotel, and I turned at the corner and headed downtown.

From an outdoor phone booth at the corner of Fourth Avenue and Twenty-fifth Street I called a man many miles away. I had heard that most pay phones in Manhattan are tapped, but I didn't really believe it could be dangerous. The police could not possibly have the personnel to listen to all of the phones all of the time. I didn't care. I got his number from Information, and I dialed it direct, hoping he'd be in his office. He was.

I said, all in a rush, "Warden Pillion, this is Alex Penn, I have to talk to you, I didn't kill that girl, I never killed anybody—"

"Where are you, Alex?"

"Chicago." Never trust anyone. "I have to—"

"You'd better turn yourself in, Alex."

"I didn't kill that girl, Warden. I was framed. I can't prove it and I can't expect anyone to believe it, but I *know* it. I saw someone else kill her just before I passed out. Damn it, I *remember* it. And—"

"The police will—"

"The police will throw me in a cell. I wouldn't blame them a bit. You don't believe me, do you?"

"Well, I—"

"No reason why you should. Warden, just let me talk a minute, that's all. I know I didn't kill the girl. Or the first one, Evangeline Grant. I never could believe that I had done it, I never remembered it, and the pattern's the same, someone must have framed me. Because there's no reason for anyone to frame me now. I'm nothing, I'm not even a person, nobody even knows me, but I used to be somebody and have things and somebody framed me then, some son of a bitch did it to me, and did it again the night before last, and—"

"What do you want me to say, Alex?"

"I don't know."

"I have to tell you to turn yourself in. You know that."

"Yes."

"Of course you don't have to do what you're told, do you?"

"Thank you, Warden."

"Be very careful. Don't expose yourself unnecessarily. And don't . . . don't do anything violent. Keep away from liquor. Am I telling you anything you hadn't figured out for yourself?"

"No."

"I thought not. For the record, I don't believe you. I think you killed Evangeline Grant, and I think you killed Robin Canelli. I think you're a very dangerous man. I have to think that, you know that."

"Yes."

"I hope that you're right and I'm wrong. Why did you call me?"

"I had to talk to someone. I'm going crazy, I had to talk to someone. I couldn't think of anyone else."

"Did it help?"

"Yes, I think so—"

The operator cut in to tell me my three minutes were up. I hung up immediately and left the booth. I wondered whether he would trace the call. It would be possible, I think; he had the operator there on the line, and it seemed probable that an operator could check the source of a long-distance call even after the connection had been broken. Would he call the New York police? Probably, if only to cover himself.

He wanted me to be innocent. He even wanted me to try to solve things on my own. Even so, he didn't believe me.

He would, though. Once I found the bastard who jobbed me, once I nailed him down, they'd all believe me.

· 8 ·

I SAT IN MY HOTEL ROOM WRITING OUT IDIOT LISTS. IT WAS AN
old habit, a hangover from my undergraduate days. Whenever I was trying to organize a paper or plan a line of research, I wrote down long lists of words and names and
phrases and focused on them like Buddha on his navel. Later
on I developed my lectures the same way. I had to have
something on paper, something I could look at and read.

*Pete Landis. Don Fischer. Doug MacEwan. Gwen. Gwen's
second husband—*

What was his name? And had he been seeing Gwen *before*
Evangeline Grant's throat was slashed? And wielded the knife
to get me out of the way?

Would a man commit murder to become head of the history department? I suppose men have killed for less. I would
have eventually become head of the department, with any
luck at all. Cameron Welles would sooner or later have retired, and it had been more or less taken for granted that I
would have his post once he left it. I was a year or two junior
to *Warren Hayden* (whose name I now added to my list) but
was publishing more, had a somewhat wider range of historical interest, and was very definitely his superior in campus
politics.

While I was in prison, and thus removed from the race, old
Cam Welles retired, to be succeeded by Hayden. So he cer-

tainly had had no reason to regret my disappearance from the scene. But did a man murder for such a reason?

And why, then, would he have done it a second time? He might have killed Evangeline Grant to frame me, but once it had worked, why on earth repeat it? Why kill Robin in the bargain? I was well out of things, no continuing threat to him. Of course he might have worried that I suspected him, that I would seek him out and obtain some strange sort of revenge, but why?

Peter Landis had gone with Gwen before I married her. The two of them had had a protracted affair, complicated, Gwen had later told me, by a false pregnancy which very nearly led them to the altar. Then they broke up, and went back together again, and broke up again, and then I met Gwen and married her.

Jealousy?

Perhaps. And perhaps she had been seeing Pete while we were married, perhaps he thought he could have her again if I were only out of the way. He was married himself by then, and Gwen and I had played bridge with the Landises, gone to concerts with them, sat up long evenings at their place or ours, drinking and talking the night away. Pete had been a customer's man with a rather good brokerage firm, and had seemed to be doing very well at it. Mary Landis was a shy thing, soft of voice and unsure of opinion, prettier than one realized at first or even second glance, with a propensity for getting slightly smashed on two drinks and passing the rest of the night in perfect silence.

Pete and Gwen. I wondered if he and Mary were still married. And if he and Gwen had ever resumed their affair. And if he might have hated me over the years, certain that he and Gwen would have gotten back together but for me.

Her new husband. Where precisely had he come from? How had she found him? Of course a vibrant woman like Gwen would not be the sort to wait patiently for her husband to finish serving a life sentence—I'd taken as much for granted, and had not been particularly astonished when she divorced me and married again. (Although, to be honest, the news had depressed me rather more than I cared to admit.)

She was an attractive woman. She could find a man easily enough. But suppose this new husband—I would really have to find out his name—had been someone she knew of old. Suppose they had been having an affair before I got framed for murder.

Why wouldn't she simply divorce me? God knows I had given her grounds, and if she knew enough to have me set up for Evangeline Grant's murder, she also knew enough to obtain evidence of adultery.

Nor could I see her as a killer, or as a party to murder. I thought of her behavior at the trial and before, and it struck me as inconceivable that she could have been faking all of that. Unless she actually knew nothing about it—

That was possible. Suppose this new husband of hers had wanted her to divorce me and marry him. And suppose she wouldn't go along with it. As far as Gwen knew at the time, she and I had a damned good marriage. If she found herself caught up in an affair, she might go along with it (just as I went and chased whores) while remaining quietly determined to keep our marriage intact.

And, if the son of a bitch was sufficiently determined, he would want to get me out of the way so that he could have her. The easiest way to do that would be by killing me, and maybe he had planned as much. He could have followed me with that in mind, followed me right up into the hotel where I'd gone with Evangeline Grant. And then, seeing me passed out and the girl so defenseless, he might have realized that he'd have to kill the girl in any case, to cover his own trail, and that he was far better off letting me live just long enough to hang for the murder.

With me a murder victim, he might have had trouble getting to Gwen; many widows turn out to be far more loyal to their husband's memory than they were to his own live self.

But with me exposed and condemned as an adulterer and a murderer, my hold on Gwen would stop—as it indeed had stopped.

I lit a cigarette and paced around the hotel room, smoking furiously. My mind had hold of the picture now. Myself passed out in post-coital alcoholic coma. And he, in the room, the door closed, knife in hand, advancing on the girl. His mind playing with possibilities, realizing that the girl must die in any case, realizing next that the girl's death was enough in itself.

And the knife flashing—

And then he must have stood at the side of the bed, the knife ready to work again, while he went over it all. If I had awakened then, the knife would have done its work. But I slept on, and he saw that it was far safer to leave things as they were, with me tagged for the murder, than to kill me in the bargain and leave the police with a killer to pursue. And so he dropped the knife, and left, and that was that.

I finished the cigarette, stubbed it out. I was out of prison now, and that must have rattled him. He had to be insanely possessive to kill for Gwen when it would have been easier in the long run to convince her to divorce me. He had killed once, and it had worked, and then I was out of prison and a threat to him.

My freedom must have tortured him. I had never tried to get in touch with Gwen after my release—masochism, after all, has its limits—but he must have worried that I would come for her eventually, and that I would take her away from him.

Or that I might work it all out in my mind, even as I was working it out now, and that he would be in danger.

While I was in prison his marriage was safe. But a technicality had freed me, and now I was once again a threat to him. As long as I was alive and free he could not rest. I might come for Gwen. I might learn what he had done. I had to be disposed of, once and for all.

And so he must have flown to New York from California, and then he must have found me. I had never attempted to make myself hard to find; it had never occurred to me that anyone might have been trying to find me, and almost everyone I knew was going to great lengths to avoid me.

He found me, he followed me. Once again he had a knife. Did he plan merely to kill me this time, cut my throat as he had cut Evangeline Grant's? He couldn't have started off by planning another frame, couldn't have known how inordinately cooperative I would be. Perhaps he just wanted to kill me, maybe faking a suicide, something of the sort.

(If I were the least bit suicidal I would not have lived this long, God knows. But the police, I am sure, would have willingly written me off as a suicide. And would have shed no tears for me in the bargain.)

He must have been following me that Saturday. And it must have delighted him when I started to drink. By then he must have grown very sure of himself, knowing that I would not spot him on my trail and that, when he made his move, I would be in no condition to do anything about it. He took his time, certainly. I wandered drunk for hours. Until at last he saw me pick up Robin just as I had picked up Evangeline Grant once before, and he trailed us to the room at the Maxfield—

The poetic justice of it must have appealed to him. Once again I had set myself up nicely for him, and once again he did not have to kill me. Easier by far merely to kill the girl, to leave me just where I had been before, and then to fly back to California while I was left with a murder rap I could not possibly shake. PLAYGIRL SLAYER DOES IT AGAIN. And doesn't get out through a loophole this time, but gets the chair instead.

Of course it didn't have to be him. It might have been any of the others on my list, each supplied with a hazy conjectural motive. But at the moment I liked the way he checked out.

There was a pattern to it all, and I could see the pattern clearly.

His name—

I had Gwen's last letter somewhere around my own room. Some masochistic impulse had made me keep it in prison, so that I could read it over from time to time to remind myself that I no longer had a wife, among other things. I couldn't remember the damned name. I paced around and smoked cigarettes and closed my eyes in an attempt to bring the letter into focus, and I couldn't get hold of it. I needed his name and address for a starting place. It was all in the letter, and the letter was in a cardboard carton full of letters and books and such, and the carton was in the closet in my apartment on East Ninth Street, and I couldn't go there, I didn't dare go there.

They would certainly have the place staked out. The police are not fools, and they know that criminals all too frequently try to go home, however unsafe it is. There was sure to be a prowl car on permanent stakeout outside my building, maybe even a cop perched on a chair in the hallway. And, even if the stakeout had been lifted or never established in the first place, there were still my neighbors to be considered. Neighbors in New York are traditionally anxious not to get involved, and those in my neighborhood have little love for the police, but I was no ordinary criminal, I was the mad playgirl slayer, and if someone spotted me there was a better than average chance that the police would be called.

Of course Gwen's sister would know. I looked her up in the Manhattan book, and there was no listing. Which meant that she had moved out of the city or married someone new or switched to an unlisted number or died—any number of things could happen in all those years.

In any event, I didn't think she would welcome me with open arms.

I left the hotel. I took a bus downtown to Tenth Street and walked east. It was dangerous, but so was sitting still, and I was impatient to get something in motion. The odds that

Gwen's husband had had anything to do with the murders were long, true. Yet as long as the possibility existed I couldn't think along any other lines. All I could do was try to remember the bastard's name.

I walked my old-man walk, and I stayed in the shadows and turned my face toward the buildings when people approached. I was half a block away when I saw the patrol car. The stakeout was in no sense a subtle one. They hadn't even used an unmarked car. A regular squad car was parked in front of my building, and there were two plainclothes cops in it.

I gave up and turned around and walked away. I got to the corner, and then I remembered the fire escape.

I circled the block and entered a tenement on Tenth Street that, with any luck at all, would be more or less opposite my own building. I got into the front door by ringing an upstairs bell, and then I got to the basement and worked my way into the furnace room at the rear. There was a window facing out on the airshaft between that building and my own. I wedged myself between the furnace and the window. I couldn't get the damned thing open and I was afraid to smash it.

Then I heard glass breaking somewhere nearby, and recognized the sound—the residents of the Lower East Side lighten their garbage disposal problem by habitually chucking empty beer and wine bottles out the window. The tinkle of breaking glass never alarms anyone.

It would take, I should think, a keen ear to distinguish between the shattering of a window pane and the implosion of a wine bottle. So I took off a shoe and smashed the window to bits. I knocked all the glass from the frame, then stood waiting, putting my shoe on once again. I listened carefully, and as far as I could tell no one had shown the slightest interest in the sound of breaking glass.

I cut my hand climbing through the window. Nothing serious, just a small shard of glass my shoe had failed to dislodge.

I found the fire escape. It ended at the second floor, out of reach from the ground, so that burglars would not be able to climb it. I stood beside it for a moment, calculating just which window was mine. Then I found a garbage can and maneuvered it beneath the fire escape. By standing atop the can, I could just reach the bottom rung of the ladder.

Somewhere another idiot threw a bottle out his window (or kicked out a basement window, as far as that goes). I gripped the fire escape's bottom rung and wondered just how much noise it would make if I swung up onto it. There was more reason to get into my place than Gwen's letter. I could change my clothes—they rather needed changing—and I could probably pick up some pawnable possessions. The sailors' ninety dollars would not last forever.

I sort of pulled and yanked and jumped, and I managed to swing up onto the fire escape. It made more noise than I'd hoped and less than I'd feared, which was fair enough. I went up a few flights. Someone came to a window and stared out but didn't seem to see me. I reached my own apartment, and I tried the window, and that window was also locked, Goddamn it.

I knocked the glass out with my shoe without first removing my foot. This time it didn't sound like a bottle smashing. It sounded far more like a window being kicked in. I climbed through, and there was noise and movement in the building below me, and I turned on a light and found that the whole damn thing was a waste of time. They had stripped the place clean. Everything I owned was gone, no doubt tucked away in a police laboratory. It seemed a waste of time to check the closet, but I did, and the carton of books and papers was gone.

I was at the window, one foot out, one foot in, when the door to my apartment flew open behind me.

· 9 ·

I WENT THROUGH THE WINDOW WHILE A VOICE SHOUTED "HALT!" behind me. I scampered down the fire escape, hoping they'd think I was nothing more dangerous than a burglar with a bad sense of direction, hoping they'd decide I wasn't worth the trouble of an all-out chase. I kept going, and the voice shouted again, and I ignored it, and someone fired what I suppose were warning shots, two of them, echoing incredibly loud in the air shaft between the buildings.

I kept on going, expecting to be shot yet never even considering the possibility of giving myself up. It was not bravery. It just did not occur to me. I kept going, and I dropped from the bottom of the fire escape and hit the garbage can, and it skidded crazily out from under me. I landed badly, one leg doubled up under me, pain flickering in colored lights. Another pair of shots, and not for warning this time. One hit the garbage can. I ran. There was more shooting, a steady barrage of it, as I ran across to the window I had kicked in earlier. None of the bullets came particularly close. It was dark, and they had to shoot almost vertically, and I suppose that helped. I dove through the window, squeezed past the furnace, raced for the stairs. The door of the super's apartment burst open in front of me and a huge Negro with a cloth cap and no shirt stepped out, blocking my way. I said, "Turk!" but of course it wasn't Turk, it wasn't anyone I had ever known.

I ran straight into him. We bounced off each other, and I made a fist and threw one enormous punch at him. If he had dodged it I am sure I would have fallen down. But he was as surprised as I, and my fist found what must have been precisely the right spot on his chin. His eyes went absolutely blank and he began falling in slow motion. I ran on, to the stairs, up the stairs, down the hall, out the door.

Running, running. I knew that I ought to stop, that I had to walk normally and melt away into the shadows, but my brain couldn't convey this message to my legs. If the police had circled the block they would have seen me, and that would have been that. But luck held. After three blocks I managed at last to turn off the running and drop into a darkened doorway. My heart was hammering and no matter how deeply I breathed I couldn't suck in enough air. I thought I was having a heart attack. I held onto the side of the building, and that didn't work, and I sat down on the stairs and went on gulping air and trying to catch my breath.

It would have been very easy to black out then. I felt it coming on, waves of dark nausea and exhaustion, working at once upon stomach and head. It was drowning me. I fought it, and clenched my teeth and took deep breaths, and I stayed on top of it, until finally everything came back to what passes for normal.

Then, when I was once again steady, I began to hear the gunshots again, to feel bullets slapping at the pavement on either side of me. I had been too busy at the time to be properly terrified. Now, after the fact, I started to shake as if palsied. I couldn't stop trembling.

Stupid, stupid. Of course the apartment was empty. Naturally the police would come and take everything away. And, even if they hadn't, my landlord would surely empty the apartment prefatory to renting it to someone else. He would hardly hold it for me. Though the rent was paid through the first of the month, he had every right to expect that I would not be back.

I walked a couple of blocks, heading uptown and west. I managed to get past a good number of bars, and when I finally entered one it was less for want of a drink than to use the men's room. I was a mess, one hand cut, the other slightly bruised, my clothes dirty from the fall. I washed my hands and face and brushed off my slacks as well as I could. I was still something of a mess, but now at least I looked presentable enough to return to my hotel without raising eyebrows.

But the shaking wouldn't quit. So on the way out I stopped at the bar, telling myself I was going to have a drink because I damn well needed a drink, and telling myself also that one drink was absolutely all I was going to have.

I took a shot of bar rye, took it neat with water back, and gagged on it but kept it down. And drank the water chaser, and had another glass of water after that, and walked out knowing that I did not need a second drink, and that, thank God, I did not *want* a second drink.

The one drink helped. It took the edge off and stopped the shaking. I walked the rest of the way to Union Square and took the subway back to my hotel.

The hotel room got to me. I couldn't sit still. I took a shower and cleaned the rest of the grime from my clothes. I almost forgot the dye and washed my hair. A little water did get on it, but no harm was done.

Then I sat around the room, and tried to look at the television set. I caught the eleven o'clock news. I didn't get much of a play this time, just that I was still being sought. They hadn't received anything on the debacle at my apartment building—perhaps the police actually thought it was a burglar and not me at all. And if Morton Pillion had told the police that I'd spoken to him, they had decided to keep it a secret for the time being.

I turned off the set and started pacing the room. I had to get started, and the night had to be the best time for it. There were people I had to talk to. I didn't want to talk to anybody, but I didn't want to sit still either. I got dressed again and went out.

I called Doug MacEwan from a pay phone. He answered, and I rang off without saying anything.

He lived with his wife and son in one of the new buildings in Washington Heights. I walked across town and took a subway up to his place. I was getting over the nervousness of being among people now. After the shower, when I looked at my face in the bathroom mirror, I looked less like me than ever before. It wasn't just the gray hair. My face looked older. In just a few days I had lived some new lines and creases into it. Ones that wouldn't wash off.

I didn't want to ring MacEwan's bell. I didn't want to give him the chance to call the police while I rode the elevator to his floor. So I waited into the shadows until a woman was opening the door, and then I moved after her, holding my hotel key in my hand. I must have looked as though I belonged, because she held the door for me. We took the elevator together, and told each other what a nice evening it was, and how we hoped it would stay warm and clear for the rest of the week. She got off at the fifth floor. I rode on up to the sixteenth, and knocked on Doug's door.

He answered it in pajamas and a bathrobe. Evidently I looked enough unlike myself to put him off balance for a second or two. Then he did a take and stepped nervously backward, and I followed him inside and closed the door.

He said, "Oh, Christ."

"I need help, Doug."

"Yes, I'll bet you do. Jesus, you look awful. Did you go gray overnight or what?"

"It's dyed."

"I thought you'd be out of town by now. Or caught. I looked all over that corner for you last night, I had the money, and I couldn't find you. What the hell happened?"

So evidently he had kept our date. I felt momentarily bad for not trusting him.

"There were cops around," I said. "I got rattled, I ran."

"You want the dough? I'll—"

"It's not important. Not right this minute." I took a breath. "We have to talk. What I said last night was serious. I *didn't* kill the girl. And that means I didn't kill the first one, either. Somebody's framing me, Doug. I've got to find out who."

"The police—"

"The police won't look any farther than me. I've got to come up with something more than what I know myself. Once I do that, then I'll go for the police on a dead run. Until then I've got to do it on my own."

"What do you want from me?"

"Information. There are things I have to know. Somebody did it to me, then somebody must have had a reason. I can only think of two reasons so far. There might be more, but I can only think of two of them. The job and Gwen."

"I don't follow you."

"They were the only two things I had that somebody might want to take away from me. My job and my wife. What do you know about Gwen's new husband?"

"Absolutely nothing. She met him in California, that's all I know."

"Oh?"

"She went out after you were sent to prison. Sublet the apartment for the remainder of the lease period, sold everything except a few things she put in storage, then took a plane to the coast. Awhile after that Kay got a note from her. We exchange Christmas cards. That's about all. She hasn't been back since then, as far as I know."

I lit a cigarette. "Suppose she knew him before."

"It doesn't seem likely."

"Nothing seems likely. What's his name?"

"I don't know. Kay would know—"

"Is she home?"

"Sleeping. She went to sleep about an hour ago." He looked down at his pajamas and robe. His feet were bare. "I was reading, just about ready to turn in myself."

"Sorry to bother you."

"Don't be silly." His eyes met mine. "I think you could use a drink. What can I get you?"

"Nothing for me."

"Well, *I* can use one, then."

He found a bottle of Scotch and carried it into the kitchen. I followed him. He filled a tall glass with ice cubes, added a jigger of Scotch, then filled the glass the rest of the way with tap water. He asked me if I was sure I didn't want to join him.

"Maybe some coffee," I said.

"Instant all right?"

"Sure."

We waited while the coffee boiled. We sat at the kitchen table, he nursing a drink, me working on the coffee.

I said, "The name."

"I don't remember it, Alex."

"Wake Kay."

"I can't do that."

"Why the hell not? Christ, Doug, I don't have an abundance of time. I can't afford to wait until things are convenient for people. The time's too short as it is."

"I can't wake her."

"Why?"

"She'll panic. She'll want me to call the police. She thinks—"

"That I'm a killer?"

He shrugged, drank, nodded. "You know women."

"The hell I do."

"Well. I don't know what to do. You really think this guy—"

"I don't think anything, but it's a place to start."

"You figure he and Gwen—"

"Uh-huh."

He got to his feet. "No. Not a chance."

"She wouldn't have to have known what he did. She could have thought it was all straight, that I really killed Evangeline Grant."

"But you figure she was having an affair with him."

"That's how it would read, yes."

He shook his head. "Not Gwen," he said.

"You sound sure of yourself."

"Dammit, I am! She loved you—"

"And I loved her. But it didn't keep me out of Evangeline Grant's bed, or too many other beds before that. People are unusual animals. They don't always do things for the right reasons. They don't always do things that make a vast amount of sense." I lit a cigarette. "I need that name, Doug."

"Kay has an address book. I'm not sure where she keeps it, but I could dig it up."

"Do that."

He sighed, set his glass down empty. "All right," he said. "Wait here."

I waited while he went off to hunt for the name and address of my wife's current husband. I waited, smoking my cigarette, drinking my coffee, listening very intently. At first I didn't realize what it was that I was listening for. Then all at once I did. I was waiting for the sound of him making a telephone call to the police. The sound never happened, and he came back with a red leather book in his hand, and I wondered when if ever I would be able to start trusting people again.

"This is it," he said.

The entry, carefully inscribed in Kay MacEwans's small neat hand, read:

> *Mr. & Mrs. Russell J. Stone (Gwen Penn)*
> *4315 Portland Hill Drive*
> *Los Angeles, California*

"She didn't take down the zip code," Doug said idiotically.

"I don't think I'll need it."

"Are you going out there?"

"God, no. Too dangerous. And not worthwhile, yet." I copied down name and address on a scrap of paper, tucked it away in a pocket. "Mr. Russell J. Stone sounds very possible," I said. "But there are other possibilities."

"Like who?"

"Like an old boyfriend of hers whom I don't think you know. Like a departmental colleague of mine whom, come to think of it, you do know. Whatever happened to Warren Hayden?"

"Hayden? You must be kidding."

"I haven't done any kidding in almost five years, Doug."

"Well, why in hell would Warren Hayden—"

"Cam Welles got put out to pasture, didn't he?"

"Oh, sure. Just a couple of months after you, uh—"

"You can say *went to jail*, you know. I know I went. There's no point in pretending it didn't happen."

"Just a few months after you went to jail, Cam Welles retired."

"And Warren got the top spot?"

"Who else was there?"

"My point," I said.

He stared incredulously at me. "Do you mean to suggest," he said, "that for the sake of a department chairmanship, a meek little man like Warren Hayden would take a knife and—"

"Why not?"

"Alex—"

"God damn it," I said, "at least it's a reason, isn't it? Everybody on earth is very goddamn willing to believe that I killed two girls for the sheer hell of it, with no reason at all. At least I'm talking about motives, I'm advancing some possibilities." I lit another cigarette. "There was an old lag I knew, a trusty in for life. A murderer. You know why he was in there?"

"No."

"He was playing cards with his best friend and he lost. And when he thought about it afterwards he decided that the friend must have cheated him, and that really got him mad. He waited two days and thought it out all very carefully, and then he went downtown and bought a shotgun, and then he went to the friend's place and emptied both barrels in the friend's face. Took most of his head off."

"I don't see—"

"You didn't let me finish. You know how much he lost in that card game? You know the staggering sum that made him kill?"

"Alex—"

"Fifteen cents, Doug." I closed my eyes for a moment. The human race is so imperfect an invention. "Fifteen cents. The chairmanship of the history department is worth a hell of a lot more than that."

"I don't think Warren Hayden would do anything like that."

"Neither do I. But I'll want to make sure."

"I don't even think he's in town this year. I think he's on sabbatical somewhere in South America. Peru, I think."

"I'll have to check. There are quite a few things I'll have to check, Doug. It's my life, you know."

"Sure."

I got up, pushed back my chair. We were uncomfortable with each other, Doug and I. I had gotten what I had come for, and we would each of us be glad to say goodbye.

"I'll go now," I told him. "Thanks for the coffee, and the conversation. And Russell Stone."

"Don't go off half-cocked."

"I won't."

"Even if Gwen was having an affair, and I don't believe it for a moment, it doesn't prove anything. Not by itself."

"Maybe not."

"So just take it easy."

"Uh-huh."

He walked me to the door. "I've still got some money set aside for you. Want it?"

I said I did. I still had some money, but I felt I couldn't have too much. There was little enough time, and I did not want to get hung up with money worries. He came back with two hundred dollars in tens and twenties.

"You'll get this back," I said.

"I expect to."

He didn't expect to. He was good enough to say so. He was my only friend in the world, and he didn't really believe me, and I didn't entirely trust him. It can be rather a lonely place, this world.

"Where can I get in touch with you?"

"No place. I've been sleeping in alleyways."

"Is that safe?"

"No. I'll find a hotel now. Maybe across the river in Jersey, I don't know. I won't be staying in any one place very long, I don't suppose. Safer to keep moving."

"Suppose something comes up?"

"Put a notice in the *Times*. The personal column. One of the standard ones. *My wife having left my bed and board, I will no longer be responsible for her debts.* There's half a dozen of those every morning, nobody ever reads them, so it'll be subtle enough. And if I see it, I'll call you."

"I wouldn't want to use my own name. Kay would be furious—"

"Oh, Christ, of course not. Make up a name. Oh, Peter Porter, how's that? *My wife Petunia having left my bed and board*—that'll do it."

"Peter Porter and his wife Petunia."

"Perfect. Easy for both of us to remember."

"Uh-huh."

We very awkwardly shook hands. He opened the door for me and waited with me for the elevator. It came, and we shook hands again, a little less awkwardly, and he went back to his apartment while I rode down to the lobby.

Peter Porter and his wife Petunia. Simpler to tell him the hotel where I was staying. But I still didn't trust him, or anyone else.

· 10 ·

ON THE SUBWAY RIDE BACK DOWNTOWN I TRIED TO THINK OF something clever to do with what was left of the night. Nothing suggested itself. The night gave me far greater freedom of movement, but one could neither drop in on people nor telephone them at that hour, so that I was left with the freedom to go anywhere and no place to go.

So I went back to my hotel and made more lists. Russell J. Stone. There had to be a way to find out something about him, but how? I would sleep on it. Warren Hayden—he did look out of the picture, it appearing highly unlikely that he would fly in from Peru, cut little Robin's throat, and then resume his search for the lost city of the Incas, or whatever men sought in the Peruvian wilderness. His actual presence in Peru would need confirmation, and I would find a way to check it out, but meanwhile he looked safe.

Pete Landis. He remained on the list with nothing I had learned to confirm him or clear him as the killer. Doug didn't know him, so there had been no point in bringing up his name.

Don Fischer. I saw his name on the list from before and couldn't imagine what it was doing there. I had bought an insurance policy from him. What did that have to do with murder? I closed my eyes and saw a pleasant-faced young man with thick glasses and thick eyebrows that had grown together to form one continuous ridge of brow. Gwen's lover? My enemy? Inconceivable on both counts.

I solemnly crossed off Don Fischer's name. And began to laugh, because the only suspect—if such a term were advised in my investigations—the only suspect thus far eliminated was a man of whom I had not consciously thought at all since first writing down his name.

Penn's progress. At this happy rate, I could spend all my days writing down the names of strangers and all my nights crossing them off again, knitting a Penelope's shawl of suspicion rather than the more purposeful tapestry of Madame DeFarge.

I put my lists away. They bored me. I turned on the television set, and watched several movies which differed each from the other by the number of times the word *late* appeared in their general titles. In the middle of one of these I turned off the set and got out of my clothes and went to bed.

"Mrs. Stone?"

"Yes."

"Good morning, Mrs. Stone. I'm Curt Amory of Industrial Research Corp. I've a few questions in regard to a survey we're preparing, and if you'll give me a minute or two of your time I'll be able to send you a free gift for your troubles. Could you tell me, for a starter, approximately how many hours a week you and your family watch television?"

"Oh, well, we watch about an hour a night, I suppose, but then I watch now and then in the day time—"

I didn't much listen. I asked a few more routine questions, a handkerchief stretched over the mouthpiece of the telephone—I had read that this changes one's voice, though I honestly don't know why it should.

Then, "Now some statistics, Mrs. Stone. How large is your family?"

"Three of us. Myself, my husband, and our son."

I hadn't known about the child.

"Are you native Californians?"

"No. I moved here about four years ago."

"And Mr. Stone?"

"Moved here ten years ago from Chicago."

"And his occupation?"

"He's purchasing director for Interpublic Chemical."

I went on, picking up a few more facts to help me trace Russell Stone. As the interview progressed there was more and more space before Gwen's answers, as if she wondered why Industrial Research Corp. was interested in such a mixed bag of trivia. Then the operator cut in to announce that my three minutes were up, and at that point my once-wife tipped.

"Who is this?"

"Thanks very much for your cooperation," I said smoothly, "and you'll be receiving your free gift in the mail, Mrs. Stone—"

"Alex? Is that you? Alex, what's going on?"

I didn't say anything.

"Who is this? Alex? I don't—"

I replaced the receiver and left the booth.

In an irrational way, I was pleased that Gwen had at last recognized my voice. After all, I had been married to the woman for quite some time. And even then, while we were married, I had occasionally found myself thinking of her as rather like those huge new glass and steel apartment buildings. One could live in one of those apartments for fifty years, and the day one finally moved out the apartment would shake itself utterly free of every trace of one's occupancy; it would be as though one had never been there at all.

So it often seemed with Gwen. I was sure I had made no impression upon her, that in the process of divorcing me she went through the rooms and corridors of her mind, wiping away any traces I might have left therein, tidying up carefully and readying the rooms for the next occupant. I found it startling, for example, that Russell Stone had been able to gift her with a child; if ever a woman were constitutionally designed to be barren, that woman was Gwen.

Perhaps they had adopted the child. I found myself wanting to believe as much.

I stopped at a Cobb's Corner and had a cup of coffee at the counter. The telephone conversation played again through my mind and I smiled at the inanity of it. A survey indeed. Market research has had an extraordinary effect upon the American public. The average citizen is so well accustomed to answering any number of idiot questions about himself that he has become quite incapable of telling strangers to mind their own damned business. Virtually anyone will reveal virtually anything about himself once he is convinced that the questions are purposeless, designed only to facilitate the waste of corporate time and money.

Would Gwen mention the call to Stone? I thought it over and decided that she probably would not. I couldn't believe she had any knowledge of the frame, and thus would not know that he had to be protected—assuming, that is, that he was guilty. Thus what she would have to say, in effect, was something like this: *I had a long distance call today, I think it was from Alex, but he pretended to be a market research surveyor and I told him any number of things about us before I guessed that it was him.*

Gwen has never enjoyed looking like a fool. Few people do. She would forget the conversation, or convince herself that it was not me after all, or some such. She would not mention it to Stone, and he would not know that I was measuring him for an electric chair. Good.

The New York Public Library showed me Russell J. Stone's face. There is a magazine, I discovered, called *Purchasing World,* a trade journal which is evidently of some interest to purchasing agents. According to my once-wife, Stone had been promoted to his present position a bit over three years ago, so I went through a stack of issues of that vintage looking for the story that would inevitably accompany such a promotion.

Patient plodding is the cornerstone of historical research. I made my boring way through the stack of issues until I finally found the article. They had given him most of a column, and there was a good head-and-shoulders shot of him, lips smiling bravely, eyes frank and open, hair neatly combed and parted. He looked like a large man, a beef and bourbon type, a little older than me, a good bit wealthier than me, a far sight more successful than me in almost every respect. Gwen, I thought, had stepped up nicely, had made a good exchange.

I read the article. There was a boring lot on what his new duties would include, and what his old duties had included, and then there was the biography of our hero, the college he went to, the fraternity, the honors, the first jobs, all the grand and glorious steps he had climbed en route to the pinnacle of success he presently occupied, purchasing director for Interpublic Chemical.

He was an Indianan, a Purdue graduate. He worked first in Pittsburgh, then for a long stretch in Chicago, and finally in California. And, almost completely hidden in the list of jobs, there was the information that he had been on special assignment for his Chicago employers for the better part of a year, the very year Evangeline Grant was murdered and Alexander Penn saddled with her murder.

Special assignment in their New York office.

I ripped that page out of *Purchasing World*, feeling as I did so that few persons beside myself were likely to have any great interest in that particular story. I, on the other hand, would want to refer to it from time to time. I had found my man. Now I would have to hang it on him. I wanted to know everything that page could teach me about him. I wanted to stare long and hard at that sleek successful face, and I wanted to coax and prod my memory until I could know where I might have seen that face before.

In my room I drew the blinds and lay on my bed in the darkness. I concentrated on that face, and then I went back to the night when it happened. The arm, the hand, the knife, all of it going for Robin while I lay there, doing nothing. I tried to match a body to that arm and put a face on that body. It seemed as though there was something about that arm that was memorable but I couldn't focus it in my mind. I invented the right sort of body for an old Purdue football player gone a little bit to fat, and I put that sleek head on top of it, and I fought fiercely to make myself remember having seen it all just that way.

But it wouldn't work. I could just about convince myself that it had happened that way, but I couldn't make it interlock with anything that remained in my memory. It was possible, I thought, that with the selective vision of the drunk, I had seen only the arm and the hand and had never seen the killer's face at all.

If that were the case, teasing my memory would do no good. I could not force myself to recall what I had never seen.

In the darkness, in the quiet, I found myself remembering Sunday morning in the Maxfield Hotel. It was now—what? Tuesday, incredibly enough. Tuesday afternoon, late afternoon.

It seemed ages ago.

I let myself remember it, the moment of discovery, all of it. And then there was something that had not bothered me before, but that seemed inconsistent now. When I wrapped myself up in the bedsheet and went down the hall to the bathroom, the door to my room had been locked. Not from the outside—you needed the key to lock that door, and the key had been in the room with me. But the door had been bolted from within, and I had unbolted it before I could leave.

Who could have locked it? Robin? It seemed logical that she would, but I couldn't remember her doing so. And if she had, how had the killer entered the room?

All right. Suppose, then, that she had not bolted the door. Then whoever killed her had somehow contrived to bolt the door after killing her, and leave without disturbing the lock. It was possible, if there was a fire escape at the window, or a door leading to an adjoining room. But why do it that way? Why not just leave by the regular door?

Of course it made a better frame this way. Finding myself locked in with her, I had to believe that I had killed her myself. But—

There was a sudden flash of horrible doubt, and I threw myself up from the bed and turned on the overhead light, unwilling to be alone in the darkness with the horrible feeling of dread.

Because—

Because suppose the memory of that arm and hand were a false memory, a schizoid separation of self from self. Suppose, then, that a part of my mind had chosen to see myself kill Robin and view it as the act of another man. Suppose—

No.

I was not going to let it be that way. No.

· 11 ·

I CALLED GWEN ON TUESDAY MORNING. BY WEDNESDAY NIGHT I
was so profoundly awash in a sea of lists and phone calls and
clippings and names that I ached for the dry land of movement and action and contact. I had to find out things about
Russell Stone, about Pete Landis, about Warren Hayden. And
I had to find out these things without exposing myself, somewhat in the manner of a smoker attempting to light a cigarette from a roaring bonfire. I didn't dare get close enough to
do the job. So far I had not gotten burned, but the cigarette
wasn't lit, either, and its end was not even warm.

Hayden was in Peru. A telephone call to the college con-
firmed this, he was on sabbatical leave in Peru, he had left
months ago, and it would be months before he would return.
The airlines which link New York with Lima had no record of
a passenger named Warren Hayden within the past month. He
could conceivably have slipped away from the lost city of the
Incas to fly to New York and back under an assumed name.
He could have done this, but I would not make book on it. I
crossed him off the list.

Pete Landis led me a chase. He wasn't listed in the phone
book at his old address, but there were other P. Landises and
Peter Landises scattered throughout the five boroughs, and I
wasted dimes calling several of them. I called his old employer and couldn't get any information about him. He wasn't

with them any more, and they either did not know or would not say where he was now. I called the main office of the New York Stock Exchange on the chance that they might keep track of the whereabouts of various brokers. I talked with a good many secretaries and assistant managerial types and got nowhere.

I called the branch post office in his old neighborhood to see if they had a change of address card on him in the files. They didn't, so I went to his building on the chance that he and Mary had de-listed their telephone number. They were not living there. I asked the building superintendent if he remembered the Landises, and when they moved. He said he couldn't keep track of everybody, and that he had only been on this job for a year and a half, and maybe they had moved out before his time. I asked if he could call the landlord and check it out for me. He didn't know if the landlord would keep records of past tenants. I told him it was worth checking out, and he said he was a busy man and had plenty of things to do.

"I'd appreciate it," I said.

"Well, it'd take up my time."

"It's important to me."

"Important is important, but time is money."

I felt exceptionally stupid. It had never occurred to me to bribe the man. I had no idea what might be the proper bribe. I handed him ten dollars, which in retrospect seemed rather high for one phone call. He did not offer to give me change. He went into his apartment and closed the door, leaving me out in the hallway. I heard him dialing the telephone but couldn't follow his conversation. I had a sudden urge to run, certain that he had recognized me and that he was calling not the landlord but the police. I lit a cigarette and forced myself to stay where I was, and a moment later he returned with an address scrawled on an irregular scrap of brown wrapping paper. They had moved three years ago, the superintendent assured me. I thanked him—why thank him? he was well paid—and left.

The scrap of paper gave me a street address in Atlanta. The Atlanta telephone operator had no listing at that address, but did have a Peter Landis listed at another Atlanta address. I got the number, dialed it direct. Mary answered. I recognized her voice, and was amused to discover that three years in Georgia had provided her with a southern accent.

The fact that the two of them were still married answered most of my questions, and made me anxious to leave it at that and cross him off the list. Still, I felt I might as well go on playing detective. I didn't want to use the market research survey now. I didn't feel I could fake a southern accent, and my own speech might not sound like the tone of an Atlanta-based researcher.

Instead I passed myself off as an old buddy of Pete's who hadn't seen him in years and was just passing through town. I don't recall what name I invented for the occasion. Mary got quite excited—her accent slipped, which pleased me—and suggested I call Pete right away. She gave me his number and the name of the firm he was with. He had a junior partnership now, she told me, and would very probably be made a full partner after the first of the year.

"Ah'm sure he'll be thrilled to heah from you," she said, the drawl firmly back in place now. "He's told me so much about you."

I privately doubted this. She asked if I would be in town long, and if I could come to dinner. I said that I was leaving in a few hours, that I had passed through town a few days ago and tried to call them then.

"I tried you on Saturday," I said. "You must have been out of town."

"Saturday? We were home all day."

"Saturday night."

"Oh. Why, we were out at the club—"

I finished the conversation and rang off, promising to call good old Pete at the office. If they were home all day Saturday and at the club all night, it seemed highly unlikely that good old Pete could have been in New York late Saturday night or early Sunday morning to slit Robin Canelli's throat.

It was unlikely anyway, since Pete and Mary were still together, and since he was evidently quite successful, and all the rest. If he had killed for Gwen, why wouldn't he have pursued her once I was out of the way?

The trouble with this, of course, was that it was all conjecture. I could make a case either way, but it could never be more than hypothesis. Perhaps he killed Evangeline Grant to frame me because he wanted Gwen, and then the shock of killing destroyed his feeling for Gwen and drove him closer to Mary—and made him anxious to leave New York in the bargain. It was possible if not probable, and though he was less a suspect than before, he had to stay on the list.

What it all came down to, in fact, was that I had to know if Gwen was seeing anyone while we were married. If she had had an affair with either Stone or Landis, he would be at the top of the list and a leading prospect. Or, for that matter, if she were having an affair with someone else, someone who had not even occurred to me thus far, someone perhaps whom I did not even know, I could then throw away my list and start over. I had to know that part of it or I couldn't possibly get anywhere.

The same thing kept hanging me up with Russell Stone. I tried to check on him, and I did in fact manage to learn quite a bit about him. I didn't dare call him, not after Gwen had recognized my voice, but I called all over New York and checked out such arcane matters as his New York residence, his previous employers, and such. It told me things about Russell J. Stone, but it did not tell me whether he had met Gwen in New York while she was my wife or in California when she was my ex-wife. And without knowing this one final fact I couldn't know whether or not he was the one.

I could find out, for example, that he had not made a recent flight to New York under his own name. This meant nothing. I could find out that his New York apartment had been several miles from our own. This, too, meant nothing. I could find out material which might have been of interest to his biographer. It was occasionally of interest to me as well. But it didn't get me anywhere.

At one point I thought of calling Gwen. "Honey? This is Alex, your once if not future husband. Look, sweetie, I know you were sleeping with somebody while I was married to you. Was it (a) Russell or (b) Pete? or (c) none of the above? Tell me, doll, because it is of great importance to me."

I didn't make the call. But I was tempted.

But it had finally gotten to be Wednesday night, and I had run out of patience at about the same time that I had learned nothing significant from the last logical avenue for exploration. I had essentially narrowed the field to one suspect, which should have been a victory for me, but it didn't amount to much. There was nothing I had learned which would conceivably make a jury deliberate an extra five minutes before finding me guilty as charged.

At yet another lunch counter over yet another cup of coffee I closed my eyes and saw again my once-wife. I focused quite intently upon the image, trying to bring back her impact upon all five senses. How she looked, her head cocked to the right when she concentrated upon something, the way her hands moved in conversation. The sound of her voice, the several words she habitually mispronounced (exquisite, for one, the middle syllable of which she accented, and which was, incidentally, her favorite laudatory adjective). The smell and taste and touch of her, and these less in a sexual sense than in the manner in which they helped to constitute her essence, her presence, the actuality of all that was Gwen.

I had spent some years as this woman's husband. It had never occurred to me, in all that time, that she might have been having an affair with someone. No doubt my vision had been obscured by my preoccupation with my own endless rounds of compulsive infidelity, stemming from some unknowable and unopposable dark need, and neatly blinding me to my mate's acts.

Had she so done? And with whom?

I realized with a measure of surprise that I had no intuitive answer to either of these pertinent questions. They had to be answered, but the answer would have to be found; I could not find it within myself. And this discovery brought quick understanding of how little I had known the woman. I had thought that I knew her, and I had been wrong. I never knew her at all.

Who did?

Certainly, if she were having an affair, someone beside her lover would know of it. As far as I knew, she did not have a friend in the world close enough to her to enjoy her confidences. But, if I could postulate an unknown lover, by the same token I could gift her with a dozen unknown and unknowable confidantes. Q.E.D.

There was one possible confidante known to me. Her older sister, Linda, whose name I had already failed to find in the phone book. Her hip sister, her brassy sister, her several-marriages-much-psychoanalysis-two-suicide-attempts sister.

Whom, unfortunately, I devoutly loathed, and who had always loathed me in return.

It wasn't late. Eight-thirty by the luncheonette wall clock. I finished my coffee and waited for a boy with girl-length hair to get done on the phone. Then I dropped my dime in the slot and dialed Doug's number. It rang twice, and Kay answered it.

I dropped my voice a notch and asked for Mr. MacEwan. This didn't work. There was a fractional pause, then, "Alex? Alex?"

"Is Doug there, Kay?"

Her voice went shrill. "You have to leave us alone, Alex! You have to leave us out of it, you can't come here, you can't keep calling us! It was years ago! Years ago—"

"Kay, I just—"

"It means nothing now, can't you understand? It's over and done with, we've forgotten all about it—"

Then the phone was taken from her, and there was some off-stage banter which I did not catch, and then Doug said my name.

What I said was, "I think Kay's secretly in love with me."

"She's a little shaky, Alex. That's all."

"Sure."

"We all are, really. What's up?"

"I have to know Gwen's sister's address."

"Huh?"

"I said—"

"No, I heard you. Hell, I don't know it. I only met her —what? Twice? Three times?"

"I don't care if you saw her on television, Doug."

"Huh?"

I made myself take a breath and hold it for a few seconds. Then I said, "You can find out for me. You can make one or two calls and get the information for me. I'm up to my neck in legwork, I can't move around, I can't even call people and ask them the answers to simple questions. You can call Gwen, I'll give you her number—"

"Don't be ridiculous."

"Listen a minute. You'll call her or you can have Kay call her, and all you have to do is ask her how to get in touch with Linda, her sister Linda. I don't know her last name now, she gets divorced every two years or so, but Gwen will know. Call now, and I'll buzz you back in half an hour and take the relay."

"Do you know what you're asking me to do?"

He had me stretched so tight that, if plucked, I would have played high C. I opened my mouth to yell at him, and realized that that wouldn't accomplish much, and realized at about the same time that I could no longer talk reasonably. So I broke the connection and went outside.

I walked around the block and called him again from a drugstore phone. This time he answered it himself. I said, "I hung up because I didn't want to shout at you. I'm asking you

to do something which no one will know about and which
will not get you involved at all. I've been going through hell
for half a week with too much to do and no room to move
around in. All I want is a name and an address and a phone
number. I can't call Gwen. You can, or Kay can. Make up
some story, you want to invite her to a party, you know a guy
who wants to meet her, anything. But if you don't make the
goddamned phone call I'm going to call the police and tell
them that I saw Alexander Penn going into your apartment,
and then see how much sleep you and Kay get tonight."

"You wouldn't do that."

"Just try me, you stupid son of a bitch."

He thought it over. Then he said, "Well, I can't guarantee
anything."

"I can."

"Huh? Oh. Well, I'll make the call, I'll see what I can find
out. It's Linda, isn't it?"

"Right."

"You have Gwen's number?"

I gave it to him.

"Should I call you back?"

"I'll call you. Half an hour."

I rang him back thirty minutes later, to the minute. He told
me what I wanted to know. He was lucky. If he hadn't had it,
I'd have set the police on him. I honestly would have done it.
It would have accomplished nothing, it would have hurt me
more than it would have helped, but I was in a black and
hateful mood, and when you don't know who your enemies
are you have to hate your friends. Any port in a storm.

• 12 •

LINDA TILLOU HAMMILL PLIMPTON CRANE HAD A NEW NAME, a new phone number, and lived in a new city, the three of which combined to make it highly unlikely that I could have found her on my own. She had been recently divorced from Plimpton when last I'd heard of her, and I now learned from Gwen via Kay and Doug that she had since married and divorced Crane, in whose Larchmont home she presently lived with Hammill's son and Plimpton's daughter.

The Larchmont train leaves from Grand Central and passes through the Hundred Twenty-fifth Street station en route to the Westchester suburbs. I weighed the relative perils of boarding at Grand Central, where cops habitually lie in wait for arriving and departing fugitives, or to be wildly conspicuous as one white face in the black sea of Harlem. Grand Central, moreover, was close enough to walk to, which gave it a decided edge. I did so, and drank coffee until they called a Larchmont train, and boarded it, and bought a ticket from the conductor.

The ride was pleasantly uneventful. Someone had abandoned a copy of the *World Journal*, and I hid behind it all the way to Larchmont. No one took undue notice of me. There was a gas station a block from the Larchmont terminal. A skinny kid there put down a copy of *Road and Track* long enough to tell me how to find Merrimack Drive. It took me about fifteen minutes to walk to her house.

A ranch house, red brick with white clapboard trim, set far back on a wide and deep lot, with a couple of postwar oak trees in front. The garage door was closed and there was no car parked in the driveway or at the curb. I checked the garage. A green MGB nestled among a sprawl of kids' toys. The obvious car for a suburban mother of two. Linda had not changed.

Either she was home alone or she was out with someone, in which case there would be a babysitter watching her young. It was somewhere between ten-thirty and eleven—I had never gotten around to replacing my purloined watch. I lit a cigarette, smoked part of it, put it out, and went to the front door and rang the bell.

There was a peephole in the door. I put my hand over it. I heard someone open the peephole for an unsuccessful reconnaisance, then Linda's voice asking who it was.

"Bela Lugosi," I said.

It was the sort of reply usually forthcoming from the sort of morons she was friendly with. The lock turned and the door opened and I got a foot in it, and she said, "You must be some kind of a—" and saw my face. Her eyes cracked and she said, "You son of a bitch," and tried to slam the door. I put a shoulder into it. It flew open. She backed away, trembling, and I kicked the door shut behind me.

She was on the tall side, taller than Gwen, but as thin and angular as a stiletto. Her hair was cut short and dyed black, then tipped silver. She had large brown eyes punctuated by tiny pupils.

"What are you doing here?"

"I have to talk to you."

"Did you bring your knife, killer?" She laughed like glass breaking. "Are you going to kill me?"

"No."

"What on earth do you want from me?"

"Information."

"You've got to be kidding."

"I'm not." She was backing away toward the door, and I

moved around her to the left to leave her no place to run. "I didn't kill that girl. I didn't kill either of them."

"I only heard about the one Sunday. Did you kill another one since?"

"I never killed anybody. Not five years ago and not now." She started to say she didn't believe me, then shut her mouth again and played Humor The Lunatic.

"I'm being framed," I said.

"Tell me more."

"Somebody set me up the first time around. It worked so well I even believed it myself. Then I got out. You know about that."

"So?"

"So they worked the frame again."

"Who did?"

"That's what I'm trying to find out."

The fear was leaving her now. Her eyes met mine, cold, brittle. There was an odd light in them. I wondered if she had been drinking.

"Do you expect me to believe all this?"

"I don't honestly give a damn what you believe. I just want some answers to some questions."

"Like what?"

"Russell Stone."

"Gwen's husband."

"That's right."

"What about him? You want to kill him?"

"No."

"He's not much. He's a stiff. Very proper, very much the company man, the Protestant ethic, that whole bag." Laughter. "Goodlooking, but I bet he's a drag in the hay. I threw a pass at him on their last trip east. He wasn't having any. I don't think he approves of his sister-in-law."

"When did Gwen meet him?"

"I don't know. You're giving me a headache, killer. You want a drink?"

"No."

"Oh, that's right. You don't drink, do you?"

"I—"

"You don't drink and you don't kill girls. You just get framed by evildoers, is that right?"

I drew a breath. "You ought to humor me," I said. "Get nasty with me and I might take after you with a knife."

"I've decided I'm safe with you, killer."

"Why?"

"I'm not a whore."

"That's a matter of opinion."

"I never sell it. I only give it away."

"That's all it's worth."

The eyes flashed. "Go easy, killer. I'm bitchier than you, you'll come out second best."

"I didn't come here to fight, Linda."

"I know. You want in-for-ma-tion."

"That's right."

"What I want," she said, "is a drink. Just a small one, because I am nicely up on bennies and too much would blunt the edge. Sure you don't want one?"

"Positive." I wanted one desperately.

"Then I drink alone." I followed her into the kitchen. She poured Scotch into a water tumbler. "Get me some ice, will you? Right behind you."

I turned toward the refrigerator, then heard her move. She was making a grab for the wall phone. She had the receiver off the hook and her finger in the "O" hole. I hit her open-handed across the face. She reeled away, and I pulled the phone out of the wall.

Her face was white, with red marks from my fingers. "Superman," she said.

"Don't try it again."

"Not with that phone, I won't." She picked up her glass. "What would happen if I threw this in your face?"

"I'd beat the crap out of you."

"Uh-huh. Well, the hell with the ice." She drank the straight

Scotch all the way down and put the empty glass on the counter. "You hurt me, killer."

"You had it coming."

"I know." She stood for a moment, thinking. "The hell with it. I don't want to get hurt any more. The killer plays too rough. I just want you to get the hell out of here. I don't suppose it would do me much good to scream, would it?"

"None."

"I didn't think so. So let's go back to the living room and sit down on the couch, and you can ask me your precious questions about Russ Stone, All-American Boy. And I will answer them and then you will go away. All right?"

"Fine."

We went back to the living room. There was a phone there, and I ripped the cord out of the wall.

"I don't think you trust me."

"I don't trust anybody."

"That's probably a good policy." She settled herself on the couch, folding her long legs under her little rump. "You want a cigarette?"

"I have my own."

We lit cigarettes. She inhaled deeply, sighed the smoke out, and shrugged. "Okay," she said. "What do you want to know?"

"I think Gwen was having an affair with someone while we were married. Whoever it was, he'd have a good motive for framing me. The only motive I can think of. I want to know who it was."

"You honestly think Gwen was playing around?"

Did I? A difficult question. "Yes."

"What makes you think that?"

"It doesn't matter. I want to know who the man was."

"Don't you have it mixed up? You were the cheater, lover."

"Forget that."

"You think my little sister—"

"Cut it out, Linda. You know all about it. Now tell me."

She considered this. "If she were having an affair," she said thoughtfully, "why should she tell me about it?"

"Someone would have to cover for her from time to time. She didn't have any really close friends in town. Except you."

"She never said anything to me."

"You're lying."

"I am?"

"Yes."

She stretched like a cat, ground out her cigarette in an ashtray. "It wasn't Stone," she said. "I'll bet on it."

"How can you be sure?"

"He was in California. That's where she met him."

"He was in New York at the time."

"He was? I didn't know that. But he wouldn't do anything with a married woman. Not that Boy Scout."

"Just because he turned you down doesn't mean he couldn't fall in love with Gwen."

"I'll ignore the dig, killer." She laughed shortly. "No, not Stone. The great Stone face. No. It might mess up his career, and it wouldn't be moral. Remember, I met the clown. He's a type, all right. Only with your own wife and only in the dark and only at night and only in the missionary posture. That's what they call it in the South Seas, did you know that?"

"Yes."

"Because only the missionaries did it like that down there. The natives liked it doggie style. Which has its points, certainly. That way you don't miss television."

I didn't say anything. She flicked her tongue over her red lips, her eyes holding mine. I pretended not to hear the murmur beneath the words or see the invitation in the pin-point pupils.

"It wasn't Stone," she said.

"Then who?"

"Probably nobody."

"I don't believe it. Was it Landis?"

"Who?"

"Pete Landis. Before we were married—"

"Oh, the rabbit!" She laughed aloud. "Not a bad guess, but no chance. She had a thing with him once."

"I knew about it."

"Sometimes a woman has a return engagement with an old love, but not this one. Not Mr. Wham-bam-thank-you-ma'am. When his wife had a premature baby, Gwen said it stood to reason. He's not your man, killer."

She changed position on the couch again, moving closer to me, twisting her body deliberately. I tried to ignore her. She was not at all pretty and she looked all of her years, and yet there was something annoyingly attractive about her. The evil accessibility, the aura of sexual skill and experience. I felt a stirring in my loins that I could not wholly will away, and she looked at me and knew it.

"She was having an affair," she said suddenly.

"She told you?"

"Not in so many words, but she was never good at hiding things from me. And I did cover for her once or twice, but that was easy enough. You never suspected a thing, did you, lamb?"

"No."

One hand fussed with her hair. "Poor baby." The hand dropped to my leg and patted me. "I never found out who was the lucky man. I got the impression it wasn't a name I would have recognized. Or you either. Someone she met in the neighborhood, that would be my guess."

I looked away. Not Stone, not Landis. Somebody, but no one she knew, no one I knew. Not the man she had later married.

Just . . . someone.

It didn't make any sense. Why kill for her and then give her up? Or, if he had thought he would get her, why kill a second time? He must have known he was safe. I had spent years in jail, and by the time I was out my wife was on the other side of the continent and married to another man, and I obviously suspected nothing, and did not even know the man, so that suspicion would be of no value to me—

Unless it was not her lover at all, but someone who just happened to hate me.

But who?

"You don't look happy, sweetie."

"I'm not."

"Poor lamb. I didn't help you, did I?"

"No."

She moved closer to me. I could smell her, her perfume mingling with the odor of sexual arousal. "Poor lamb," she said again, "there ought to be something I can do for you. I can't give you a drink, I can't give you any worthwhile information—"

I couldn't say anything, or move. Or ignore the dismaying fact that I wanted her.

She stood up, more bright-eyed than ever, her tongue working nervously with her upper lip. She took off her blouse and slacks, kicked off her house slippers, removed her underwear. Her body was boyish, with tiny breasts and narrow hips, and it had aged well.

"There is *something* I can give you, lamb."

I hate you, I thought, but I couldn't make the thought stick. Lust is the ultimate legislator, and the mind its servant. I stood up. I removed my own clothing. And she watched me, her eyes examining my body, saying silently that they had seen all of the male bodies in the world, and that, now, they wanted this one.

I reached for her. She danced lightly away from me, eyes amused.

"Not here, lamb. We don't want to stain the couch, do we?"

She took my arm. Her hands were cool. We walked, side by side, toward the bedroom. She bumped her hip against me as we walked. At the doorway I grabbed her, kissed her. She ground her body against mine, then slipped out of my arms.

"Bed," she said.

She lay on her back. My hands touched her breasts, her belly. I moved over her, ready for her, and . . .

"Come on, lamb. I never fucked a killer before. Can you do it without a knife, baby?"

The words were knife enough. They went for the groin and found their mark, and desire dropped like a fast curtain. Everything turned to flashes of red and black. I had a fire in the back of my skull. My hands turned to fists.

I did not kill her, I did not even hit her. I wanted to. I ached to. But somehow I found strength I never even knew I had, and I threw myself away from her, threw my whole body away from her and off the bed and onto the floor. And lay there for a nearly blank moment while the red and black faded slowly out and the world, for better or for worse, came back into focus.

"Well, Gwen said you were a lousy lay, killer. Do you always crap out like that? Is that what happens with the whores? You use the knife when you can't get it up?"

"I never killed those girls," I said quietly. I got up from the floor. "I never killed anyone. But just now I came within two inches of killing you, Linda. I hope you got your kicks."

"I got all the kicks you could ever give me, killer."

I looked at her. I couldn't even hate her any more. It was all gone, and I felt nothing more than a nugget of shame for having briefly wanted her.

"You can put the knife away," I said. "I just became immune to you."

"You think so?"

"I know so."

"My baby sister had a lover."

"I don't care."

"She told me all about it."

"I don't care."

"She wasn't in love, though. It was purely for sex. You couldn't keep her happy in that department, killer."

I turned away from her. I walked back into the living room and she followed after me. I got dressed. She didn't.

"I know who it was."

I didn't ask his name. Partly because, at the moment, I don't think I really cared. Partly because I had the feeling she would tell me anyway. I had challenged her to stick the knife in again, and she had to prove she could do it, so she would tell me.

"Don't you want to know?"

"What's the difference?"

"It was someone you know."

I dressed slowly and deliberately. I wanted more than anything on earth to get out of there and away from her, but I took my time and dressed slowly and carefully, turning my socks right side out, before putting them on, knotting my tie neatly, all of that.

And she said, "It was Doug MacEwan."

· 13 ·

I DISAPPOINTED HER. SHE WANTED A REACTION AND I SIMPLY didn't give her one. Not, I must admit, because I was too drained and dispassionate and dull to be surprised, but because I very simply did not believe her. It was too obvious a line.

"You really are immune, aren't you?"

I nodded.

"My mistake, then. I should have told you in bed. That was my Sunday punch; I was saving it from the minute you started asking, and I thought I'd hold it right until the end, but—"

"Earlier," I said, "I might have believed it."

She took a step back, placed her hands on her hips, and flashed me an astonished smile. "Oh, beautiful," she said. "You don't believe it?"

"Of course not."

"Then maybe you're not immune after all."

"You're wasting your time, Linda."

"Am I? Okay, killer, let me cite chapter and verse. Easter time, the same year you killed the girl, Gwen told you she was going with me to see Uncle Henry, who was supposed to be dying. He wasn't. The same weekend your friend MacEwan had a convention in St. Louis. He didn't. You can even check all of this out, you silly bastard. About a week after their weekend Gwen didn't come home one night. She said she was with me; I was drunk and trying to kill myself. You offered to come over and she wouldn't let you. MacEwan had a story for Kay that night, too. Then a week after that—"

She went on, and she documented everything quite perfectly, and after a while I stopped listening. I felt strangely numb. I wanted to go away. I wanted to be alone someplace dark and quiet and warm.

"Still think you're immune, killer?"

I looked at her. "Get dressed," I said. "You look lousy naked."

"I asked you a question."

I turned from her, walked toward the door.

"Do you think he framed you?"

"I don't know."

"You just can't admit that you killed those girls yourself, can you?"

I didn't answer. I didn't say anything. I opened the door, I walked outside into fresher air, I closed the door after me. And walked down the path to the sidewalk with the sound of her laughter ringing metallically in my ears.

I must have walked around blindly. I thought I was taking the right route back to the train station, but evidently I made a wrong turn somewhere and wound up lost. By the time I realized this my sense of direction was completely out of whack, and I ultimately circled around half the city and came up behind the railroad terminal from the far side.

Which was just as well.

Because I had made one mistake. I had never thought to rip the bedroom telephone out of the wall, or to incapacitate Linda, and she had decided to use the knife one final time. There were police cars all over the place.

· 14 ·

I SLIPPED BACK INTO THE SHADOWS, TURNED THE CORNER, WALKED quickly away. The train was clearly out, and it stood to reason that the bus depot would be similarly guarded. The highways out of town would be patrolled, and if I tried to hitchhike a cop would pick me up.

The gray in my hair would not help. Linda had no doubt described my current appearance when she sounded the alarm. I turned another corner, leaned against the trunk of a tree and tried to catch my breath. A wave of bright fury came suddenly and went as suddenly. I thought of going back to her house and getting her car keys, but it stood to reason that the cops would have her place staked out for the next few hours, and perhaps throughout the night. Even if they didn't, she would know better than to open her door a second time.

I kept walking. It did no good to hate Linda, I realized. One might as logically hate a cat for killing birds. It is part of the essence of catness to slaughter warblers, just as it is part of the essence of Lindaness to decorate the walls of her psychic trophy room with male genitalia. It is a trait of the species; however deplorable, one can expect no better.

I moved steadily away from the center of town and walked in darkness down quiet residential streets. Every family seemed to have two cars, and often only one was kept in the garage, sharing that space with bicycles and toys and power lawn mowers and such. The second car, ungaraged, was parked either in the driveway or at the curb.

Many of these cars, I discovered, were not locked.

This was an interesting revelation, but I wasn't sure just what I could do with it. There is a way of starting a car without a key, I understand; I believe it involves the use of some apparatus called a jumper cable or wire or something which is affixed to the terminals of the ignition switch. I'm not quite sure how it goes, and have no idea how one does it.

It would seem an art worth knowing. All of those unlocked cars began to drive me to distraction. Better by far if the cars were locked up tight with their keys left in the ignition. Any fool can break a window.

Hide-A-Key—

I remembered, suddenly, the brilliant little device sold through the mails and at hardware stores and gas stations, a magnetized box in which a spare key could repose beneath a fender, theoretically available whenever needed. I'd bought one myself once, years ago, and had dutifully tucked an extra key into it and slapped it onto the underside of a fender. It was months before I needed it, and sometime during those months it had fallen off and was lost forever.

Did people still use them? I wondered. And I checked a variety of cars, looking in the logical places, on the undersides of the fenders, front and back, and felt foolish the first time, and felt like an idiot by the time I was key-hunting on the tenth or twelfth car. But ultimately I found a year-old Plymouth convertible whose owner had responded to the Hide-A-Key sales pitch. He had evidently bought the thing about the same time he had bought the car and had never touched it since. The Hide-A-Key was rusted and grime-covered. But it slid properly open, and the key fit quite neatly into the ignition.

I had not driven in a long time, and did not know the roads. Driving—like swimming, like love—is never forgotten. Routes are, but once out of town I followed the New York markers and got where I was going. There were things I did not want to think about on the way. I played the radio, and between the noise of a rock'n'roll station and the unknown route and unfamiliar car, I didn't have to think about very much of anything.

I left the car somewhere on the West Side and walked back to the hotel. I spent the night not sleeping. I wanted a drink badly. But by the time I had managed to decide to get up and go out and have one, it was four o'clock and the bars were closed. So I stayed where I was, and kept trying to sleep, and kept not making it.

According to my erstwhile sister-in-law, Gwen had had an affair with Doug MacEwan. Linda, certainly, was in no sense constitutionally incapable of falsehood; her only reason for telling the truth instead of a lie would be that the truth was more damaging. In this case, the truth seemed to be that the pal that I loved stole the gal that I loved—and, given the circumstances, my own position seemed perfectly obvious.

Except that things are rarely as simple as they seem. The automatic rage, the sense of having been cruelly used and ignominiously betrayed, just wouldn't come. Time does more than heal wounds. Time can, in some instances, grow scar tissue in advance and prevent the wound from doing more than scratching the surface.

You see, there were all of those years in the way. The gal that I loved was a gal I loved no more. It had all happened five years ago, five desperately long years ago, and my world in those five years was so much changed that I could not put the betrayal into context. The participants in the drama were my once-wife (who now betrayed me nightly, or however frequently their schedule permitted, with yet another man, to whom she happened to be lawfully married) and my vestigial best friend, whose world now barely overlapped with mine and with whom I could no longer communicate. I might damn them both for treachery and lechery, but I was so far removed from the realness of it that I was more struck by the fortuitous rhyme of those two sins than by the awesome enormity of the crime.

I believed that it had happened. I knew that it had happened. Viewed from my present vantage point, armed with Linda's passed-along knowledge, much of Doug's reticence ever since Sunday night came vividly into focus. And, more to the point, I remembered what Kay had said, albeit hysterically, earlier that evening.

You have to leave us alone, Alex! You have to leave us out of it! It was years ago! It means nothing now, can't you understand? It's over and done with, we've forgotten all about it—

At the time I had read all of this as meaningless hysteria which defied proper translation. Forgotten all about what? And what was over and done with? Our mutual friendship, I had assumed at the time. But it now seemed clear that Kay had thought I had known of the affair—as she herself had evidently long known of it.

So I believed it. I believed it, and lay in bed not sleeping, and tried to be furious about it all, and couldn't. Which is not to say that I felt nothing. What I did feel, actually, was double-barreled—on the one hand, an alarming sense of extreme personal isolation; on the other, the sort of feeling a child must have upon discovering, many years after the fact, that he was adopted. The equilibrium-shattering realization that the most important persons in one's life are not at all what one has forever thought them to be, and that one's life itself is not as one has seen it.

Around the time that the sun came up it occurred to me that I had solved everything. Doug was Gwen's phantom lover; thus he was my phantom killer as well, and had murdered twice to frame me. I thought about this for quite some time, turning it this way and that in my mind. It seemed wholly logical at first, but of late so many things were showing themselves to be rather less logical than they first appeared. I had taken it for granted that, if Gwen had had a lover, he and the killer were the same man. Now, the more I thought it over, the more I was forced to conclude that I was working upon an equation with two unknowns. X was the lover and Y was the killer, and there was no reason to conclude that $X = Y$. Now, with X known, it seemed less and less likely.

The affair did not seem to have been a grand passion. It had ended, and must have done so in such a way that Kay MacEwan (a) knew about it and (b) did not deem it ample justification for leaving her husband. It could, conceivably, have moved Doug to frame me for murder. And, that accomplished, he could have decided that he did not want Gwen after all, that he had to stay with Kay, or whatever.

But, after it was all five years dead, after Gwen was married to another man and three thousand miles away on the other side of the country, why would Doug set me up a second time? He, more than anyone else, still knew me. He, more than anyone else, knew that I had not the slightest suspicions about anything, that I was convinced of my own guilt for Evangeline Grant's murder, that I entertained no dreams of clearing myself, that I wanted only to tread water and stay afloat one way or another. He could have had a reason for the first murder, albeit a shaky ill-founded one. But for the second murder he had no motive that I could possibly imagine.

Of course Gwen could have had more than one lover. Despite what Linda had said, there was no way to rule out Russell Stone entirely. And Pete Landis, for all her slander, might yet be the man. And—

Sand castles. Speculation.

That was all it was, all of it. I wasn't getting anywhere. I was unused to detection, and while my tactics were not without occasional skill, my strategy was amateurish and hazy at best. I knew a good many things, some of which I might have been better off not knowing, but I still had no real idea who might have killed Robin, or why.

I fell asleep somewhere around mid-morning. I dreamed an idiot dream of a girl with three blue eyes, the third one slightly smaller than the others and set just between the other two over the bridge of the nose. She kept talking to me, and the middle eye kept blinking. I woke around six with the dream still buzzing in my head, and bothering me. I couldn't get the image out of my mind. It hovered for hours. I tried to remember what the rest of the girl looked like, but I couldn't get past the extra eye. That was all that remained of the dream.

I was back in the afternoon papers again. They had begun to lose interest in me, which in turn had permitted me to feel somewhat safe walking the city streets, but now Linda had given them a fresh and exciting story, however little relationship it may have borne to reality, and I was back in print once more. My disappearance from Larchmont had not yet been explained officially. If the police had guessed that I had stolen the Plymouth convertible, or if it had been discovered where I parked it, the New York *Post* was as yet unaware of the fact.

I had dinner, then took the paper back to my room and read all of it. I threw it away and tried to decide where to go next, and what to do. I had spent a few days with an abundance of things to do, and now I was fresh out, and it unsettled me.

It was a combination of a number of things, I think, that ultimately got to me. The newspaper article, and the reality of the near capture in Larchmont, left me very shaky. I was afraid to leave the room and at the same time found myself developing an unaccustomed sense of claustrophobia, as though the room were a cul-de-sac in which I could be easily captured at any moment. I had nothing specific to do, and wanted more than ever to do something. Around eleven o'clock I left the hotel and wandered over to Times Square.

The girls were out already on Seventh Avenue, though not in full force. They mostly walked, although a few lurked in doorways or pretended to study movie posters. A collection of immaculately dressed Negro pimps grouped in front of the Forty-seventh Street Whelan's and defined the word *cool*. Uniformed cops oversaw and ignored everything. A pair of sailors picked up a pair of hookers. I kept in the shadows, had a papaya drink at the Elpine stand, worked my way through a pack of cigarettes.

I was afraid to work into the scene. The girls who were here now had very probably been on the street Saturday night. They probably knew Robin, and some of them may have seen me pick her up. They could recognize me. The cops—and there were usually plainclothes bulls on that stretch, along with the ones in uniform—would be more tuned to my picture and description than the average cop in another part of the city. It was a dangerous place for me, and yet it exerted a special fascination.

I was halfway back to my hotel before I figured out why.

I was coming at things from the wrong direction. I was getting nowhere because I was looking for motive, and as a result was flying blind. There was more to it than motive. There was fact, there was empirical observation, there was the gradual compilation of important data. I had passed up all of that by concentrating on theory. I had spent all my time trying to reason out who might have wanted to frame me for murder, when I might better have worked with clean facts to find out who actually did the job on me.

Those whores and those pimps knew Robin. Those whores and those pimps could have seen me pick her up.

And they could have seen him, too. They could have seen him following me, and following Robin and me to the Maxfield. They could know what he looked like, how he was dressed.

That was the sort of knowledge I had to tap. The police could have gotten it themselves if they hadn't closed the books on the case almost before it opened. But, convinced beyond doubt that I was the killer, they had no reason to look any further. And whores and pimps and junkies do not seek out police with their information. If they did know about the other man, that knowledge would remain hidden. I could be arrested and tried and convicted and executed, and no one would rush forward to tell the court that I was innocent, that another man had trailed us both and used the knife on Robin's throat.

They wouldn't tell the police, because the police would never think to ask them.

But they might tell me—

I thought of moths and flames. If there was one part of New York that was dramatically unsafe for me, it was those few blocks. The idea of approaching a girl, of starting to ask questions, was absolutely terrifying. She would run, or shriek, and the police would move in, and the game would be over. PLAYGIRL SLAYER CAUGHT ON THIRD TRY, the tabloids would jubilantly announce, and crime reporters would murmur darkly about killers returning to the scenes of past crimes, while somewhere a two-time murderer would relax and grin while the noose tightened around my neck.

If only I had a ticket to that world. If only I knew someone, so that I could come on like something other than a John.

I found a phone, and a phone book. There was no listing for Williams, Turk. His straight name was Eugene, and there were around fifteen Eugene Williamses listed, the greater portion of them with Harlem addresses. There were also E Williamses, any one of which might have been the Turkey.

I changed a couple of singles into dimes and went right through the list of Eugenes. I asked everyone who answered if I could speak to Turk, and eight times running I was told I had the wrong number. Did they happen to know a Eugene Williams nicknamed Turk or Turkey? No, they didn't.

The ninth time, he answered. I wasn't sure the voice was his. I asked for Turk, and he said, "Right here, man."

I said, "This is—" and stopped, because it occurred to me

that heroin wholesalers might have their phones tapped. "This is the Fountain," I said. That had been his name for me, coined when I helped him with his appeal. He had told me how brilliant I was, and I agreed I was a regular fount of knowledge, and he said yeah, a Fountain Penn.

"Mr. Ball Point."

"Right."

"Give me a number, this phone's dirty."

I did, and he rang off. I held the hook down with one hand and kept the receiver to my ear, miming a conversation to justify my continuing presence in the booth. Five or ten minutes later the phone rang.

He said, "I'm in a booth now, but let's leave out the names, dig? My man, I thought you was in Brazil by now."

"I'm here in New York."

"Well, we better do something about that. Why you called, huh? My pleasure. You got me out of a tighter place than New York, New York, and if I can return the favor—"

"Turk, I—"

"You need money and you need transportation, am I right? Money is no problem, and there's a car I can let you have. You want me to meet you some place, say where and when. I would say Mexico would be the best place for you. At least for a start. I can tell you where to hit the border, and once you're across—"

"Turk, I didn't kill her."

He stopped in mid-sentence. He was silent for a moment, then, "Tell me more, baby."

I went through it as quickly as I could. "The cat who killed her," he said finally. "You recognize him if you saw him again?"

"All I remember was an arm. An arm and a hand."

"Recollect what it looked like?"

"Like an arm, that's all. You see one arm—"

"No, hang on. Like was it a fat arm or a thin arm, or what kind of shirt on it, or was it white or colored. Dig?"

I tried. "No," I said, finally. "All I really know is that it wasn't mine. I can't do any better than that."

"You can't come any closer? It could even be a woman?"

"For all I know. I hadn't thought of that, but—"

"Yeah, I'm hip. Maybe it'll come clearer for you, maybe—"

"It won't. I've been over it too many times. I can't get any more out of it, and I'm afraid I never will."

"That does make it rugged, man."

"I know."

"So where do you go from here?"

I told him my idea of tackling it from a new angle, trying to make contact with a girl who might have known Robin. He wasn't very encouraging. "They don't talk," he said. "And you know, junkies, they never notice anything anyway. And when they do they forget it, or they won't talk about it."

"I thought you might know some of them."

"Not that crowd. I'm uptown, you know—"

"I know."

"—And down there is another scene entirely. I'll lay it out straight, baby. You're innocent and it's good for you to know it and all, but stick around this town and they'll do you just as bad as if you were guilty. Either way you got to put some mileage on you. Then maybe something comes to the surface while you're gone, and then you come back. But meanwhile—"

"I think I'll keep trying."

"Your life, man. Need anything?"

"No."

"You do, you know where to shout. Anytime, and for anything."

"Thanks, Turk."

"'Cause I owe you, you know, and I settle up."

I rang off, left the booth. I wondered whether or not he believed me. And then, hopelessly, I realized that he did not even care. His was a practical mind, cool and calm, and he saw clearly enough that I was in precisely the same bind whether it was my hand or another's that killed Robin Canelli. And his advice was correspondingly practical. Run, run, save yourself—

I found a liquor store and bought a fifth of rye.

In the hotel room I set the bottle on top of the dresser, unopened, and stared at it, and tried to find something else to look at, and thought of Linda and Gwen and Doug and pimps and whores, of girls with three blue eyes, of girls with scarlet throats.

If I was going to drink, that in and of itself was acceptable. I could survive one night in a stupor. I could even endure the blackout and hangover which would inevitably follow a bout of heavy drinking. But I was terrified that I might leave the hotel. I had to stay where I was, and when I drink I tend to roam, and when I roam I tend to wind up on Times Square, and I did not want this to happen.

I got completely undressed and tied all of my clothes in tight knots. Everything, pants, shirt, underwear, everything. I looked at them and thought that what was done could be too easily undone, that I might untie them again while drunk. I was going to soak them in the tub but decided that was silly, I would need them when I awakened, so I compromised by shoving them far under the bed where they would be hard for a drunk to get at them.

I didn't think I would try to leave. I was not, after all, the totally irresponsible drunk I had thought myself to be. I had not killed those girls. I had gone with them, as I had gone with others; this was a lamentable human failing, perhaps, but hardly a rare one, nor was it the exclusive province of drinking men.

I might be crazy. But I was certainly not stupid. I would not walk naked out of my hotel room. I would drink, I would get drunk, I would sleep it off. And, just in case I wanted to roam, there were knots in my clothing to slow me down and give me a chance to change my mind.

I picked up the bottle. I broke the seal, twisted the cap free, sniffed the contents. I got a water glass from the bathroom and filled it halfway.

I shook my head, and put the glass down untouched beside the bottle on top of the bureau. And sat down on the bed, and closed my eyes, and saw the girl from my dream with the three blue eyes. I got a chill, and began to shake.

Hell.

I got the glass, and drank the whiskey, and filled the glass again.

· 15 ·

I AWOKE WOOLLY-TONGUED BUT CLEARHEADED, IN BED, A PILLOW under my head, the blankets covering me. I got up. My clothes were still under the bed, still tortured by knots. I had evidently made no attempt to untie them and leave the room.

There was a bit of whiskey left in the bottle. I poured it down the sink and put the empty bottle in the wastebasket. I unknotted my clothes, a difficult enough task now and one which would have been impossible for a drunk, and put them on. The cure seemed worse than the disease; my clothes looked as though they had been slept in by the India Rubber Man at Coney Island.

I took them off again and spread them out on the bed so that they would have a chance to return to their original shape. I showered and shaved and dressed again and went outside for breakfast. It was a little past noon. I had evidently had quite a bit of sleep, but I had no idea when I stopped drinking and went to bed. I had a hole where my memory was supposed to be. It was fairly evident that I hadn't done anything and hadn't gone anywhere, but I couldn't remember much that had happened after the second drink. The alcohol washed the rest of it away.

I picked up a copy of the *Times*. There was a lengthier version of last night's *Post* story, and a report that the Plymouth had been found with my prints on it. Fast police work. They knew now that I was back in Manhattan.

In the personal column, there was a legal notice stating that, his wife Petunia having left his bed and board, Peter Porter would no longer be responsible for her debts. I wondered what on earth Doug wanted. He didn't figure to be home, but I decided to waste a dime finding out.

He answered the phone himself. He said hello, and I said hello, and there was a click somewhere as someone picked up an extension.

He said, "I had a call from your sister-in-law. She told me what she told you."

"So?"

"Alex, I've been sick about it for years. It just happened. Kay and I were having some rocky times, and Gwen, there was always a strong attraction, it just happened, I don't—"

"I'm right around the corner," I cut in. "Okay if I come up?"

"Sure. Sure, you come right up, Alex."

I broke the connection before the cop in the other room could trace the call. He was afraid of me, I realized. Sufficiently afraid to help set up a police trap. I left the booth in a hurry in case they had managed to run a trace in the few seconds we were talking.

I headed back to the hotel. I saw two soldiers in khaki, and somewhere a bell rang. I thought *soldiers, soldiers,* and something filtered in from the emptiness of last night's blackout. I don't know where the original thought came from. Perhaps the memory of the three sailors I had victimized in the Village, perhaps the sailors I'd seen last night on Times Square. Whatever the original impetus, I'd worked up a plan in the gentle sea of last night's whiskey, and these two soldiers had brought it back to me.

In my room, I stripped down again and got under the shower and washed all the gray out of my hair. I left the hotel, waiting by the elevator until the desk clerk was busy with someone else, then crossing the lobby in a hurry. I found a barbershop three blocks away and got a crew cut.

I let my fingers do the walking through the yellow pages, and then I let my feet do the walking to a theatrical costumer on West Fifty-fourth Street a few doors from Sixth Avenue. I told a longhaired large-eyed girl that I was supposed to be a major in a PTA play and that my old army uniform didn't seem to fit me any more.

"I see," she said. "What's the play?"

"Oh. Uh, it was written by one of our members. It's an original work. A light comedy, really."

"Would you want a dress uniform or a field uniform or what, exactly?"

I wasn't sure what army officers wore on leave in New York. Civilian clothes, probably. "A dress uniform," I said.

"I don't know if I have the right insignia for a major."

"Just so it comes close," I said. "This is just an amateur show, after all."

"I see."

She went away and came back with a uniform. It fit almost perfectly, and looked better than my own wrinkled clothes. We found an officer's cap in my size. I checked myself out in the mirror and decided I looked fine. It was still me inside the clothes and cap, but I somehow looked entirely different.

"When will you be doing the play?"

"Tuesday night."

"Dress rehearsal Monday?"

"Yes."

"Then would you want to pick it up Monday afternoon? I'll reserve it for you."

I hadn't thought of all this. The girl asked questions I hadn't anticipated, and I was poor at thinking on my feet. "I'd better take it now," I said.

"But then you'll have to pay a whole week's rental, and you won't really have any need for the costume until Monday night—"

"I don't get into New York very often."

"Couldn't someone pick it up for you? After all, it's senseless for you to be stuck for rental charges when you're not using the costume—"

I blundered through the conversation, eventually taking the tack that I wanted to wear the costume through the non-dress rehearsals as well in order to get the feel of the role. I think I only succeeded in convincing her that I was slightly crazy, but she did see that I wasn't going to change my mind. With a sigh she packed up the uniform and wrote out receipts and took my deposit—a large one, perhaps because I had convinced her of my mental instability. I gave my name as Douglas MacEwan out of sheer stupid inability to think of an alias promptly. It could have been worse; I could have said I was Alexander Penn. I went away with the uniform under my arm in a large cardboard box, and she went away shaking her pretty head.

I changed my clothes in a cubicle in the men's room of a Forty-second Street movie house. I locked myself in, got out of my clothes, got into the uniform, settled the cap on my head, and packed the old clothes into the box. I was going to abandon them there, but the box had the costumer's name and address on it, and my clothes had the labels and laundry marks that always mean so much to cops on television, so that course seemed dangerous. I left the theater and found a locker in the subway station. For a quarter I locked the clothes up. There was a notice stating that all lockers would be opened after twenty-four hours. I didn't believe this, but I didn't want to leave anything to chance, so I took the box with me—the clothes alone couldn't tell them much. I stuffed the box in a trashcan and went back to Forty-second Street.

I felt as though everyone was staring at me, and I was sure I was doing something wrong. I dreaded running into some real soldiers and being saluted by them. I was sure I wouldn't return the salute properly, or would otherwise find a way to reveal myself as an impostor. I forced myself to walk in a properly military manner, head back, spine ramrod-straight, shoulders set, covering the ground with long firm strides.

After all those days of slinking along in the shadows, it was difficult to force myself into the role.

I went to another movie. It was mostly empty at that hour. I sat in the balcony and worked my way through a pack of cigarettes.

Uniforms are masks. Nobody recognizes a mailman in his off-duty clothes. All along they've seen the uniform first and the man within as no more than a supplementary decoration for the uniform. So it stood to reason that it would work the other way around just as well. If a uniformed man was hard to recognize in civilian clothes, then a civilian ought to become invisible when he put on a uniform. That, at least, was the theory, evidently worked out while under the merciful influence of alcohol, and somehow remembered the next day.

If I was going to get closer to the killer, I had to find out what the hookers knew about it, what one of them might have seen. I had to be able to roam Whore Row after midnight. I had to look as though I belonged there, and I had to look quite unlike Alexander Penn.

I sat in the balcony and worried a cigarette and began inventing some background material for myself. My name, my rank, my serial number. My outfit. My military experience. Where I was stationed. Such things.

It didn't work. I was not an actor, and however elaborate a façade I worked up for myself, I was sure it would crumble at a touch. I gave it up and remained Major Anonymous. If anyone questioned me, if anyone suspected me, I would just turn around and run.

· 16 ·

THE PIMP'S EYES NEVER MET MINE. HE WALKED TOWARD ME
and past me and never looked directly at me. As he drew
abreast of me he said, "Nice young girls, General." His voice
barely carried to my ears. I kept walking and so did he.

A few doors uptown from the Metropole a heavyset Negro
girl flashed me a quick glance and a quicker smile. I started to
slow down, then changed my mind and kept going.

It was a little past three o'clock in the morning. It was
Friday night—or, more precisely, Saturday morning. Things
start later on the weekend. I had taken a reconnaissance walk
around midnight, and the streets were too full of tourists and
teen-age couples fresh from the Broadway movie houses. Now
the crowds had thinned way down. By four, when the bars
closed, Seventh Avenue would be reduced to buyers and sel-
lers and cops. Everyone would be there for a reason, and
everyone else would know what it was.

I lit a cigarette. My fingers shook, and after I shook out the
match I watched the trembling fingers with clinical interest. I
wondered what was shaking me up. It wasn't the uniform. I
had been walking around in it for enough hours to make me
quite accustomed to it, if not entirely comfortable in it. My
performance as Major Breakthrough (whose comrades in
arms include Private Bath, Corporal Punishment, and General
Nuisance) had improved somewhat.

What had me on edge, I realized suddenly, was this scene and my role in it. It was something new for me, strangely enough. I had been here before, I had played the John before, but I had never done all of this without the superego well muffled by alcohol. I was now almost painfully sober. I had had nothing more exhilarating than coffee in perhaps twenty-four hours. And this was the first time I had ever attempted to pick up a hooker without having first picked up and knocked off a number of 86-proof hookers well in advance. I was bride-nervous, and all of it at the one time when my interest in the girls' profession was purely academic. The discovery was as amusing as it was annoying.

I walked the street and so did they. The pimps mostly lurked in doorways, saying *young girls, party girls, sporting girls* in their soft voices. I avoided them. Many of them were likely to be Murphy men, con artists who would try to do unto me as I had done to the silly sailors in Greenwich Village. The legitimate ones might actually have girls stashed in apartments or hotel rooms, but those were not the girls I wanted to see. If they weren't on the street now, they weren't on the street when I picked up Robin, and they wouldn't be able to tell me anything.

The hookers, in their turn, said nothing at all. Some glanced my way or smiled or winked, but most of them merely kept walking and gave no sign that they knew I existed. Some had the blank dead stares of addicts junked up to the eyes, and their boneless shuffle matched the stares. Others simply looked like women, dressed neither well nor poorly, inexpertly but not wildly made up. In other surroundings one would make no quick judgments about them, but in that neighborhood at that hour their calling was instantly obvious.

But they were not aggressive. They would not solicit, they would not beckon, they would not wiggle and mince and coax. They would wait until they were approached, and I, walking back and forth, pounding the pavement from Forty-sixth Street to Fifty-first and back again, looked at each one several times over and each time passed them by.

The cops didn't worry me at all, oddly enough. The beat patrolmen were there to make sure that everything remained cool. It was not their job to harass the hookers or intercede between them and their tricks. The vice squad bulls could do this if someone downtown told them to. The uniformed cops walked their rounds, ignoring the girls as steadfastly as the girls ignored them in turn. They looked my way now and then, as I walked past them, but they never really looked at me. Their eyes focused somewhere twenty-odd feet over my left shoulder. They saw an army officer looking for a girl, filed the image into the appropriate mental pigeonhole, and forgot me forever.

I walked, I watched, I waited. I saw other men pick up girls, though this did not happen as frequently as the girls may have wished. I bided my time, painstaking though impatient, sizing up the girls and trying to make a choice. I ruled out the Negro girls, who constituted perhaps sixty per cent of the available talent. I did this for the same reason, in a sense, that I was masquerading as a soldier. Race is its own sort of uniform, and the colored hookers would be less apt to have known Robin well, less apt to have noticed when I picked her up, and less likely to have paid any attention to the man who followed us to the Maxfield. I felt, too, that they would be less willing to talk to me, but I was not so sure of this.

I also ruled out the girls who were very obviously junked up, the ones who moved over the pavement like walking death. And the very old ones, who, I felt, had less in common with Robin and would not be likely to have known her well.

It was some time before I realized just what it was that I was doing. I was shopping, just as I had shopped often enough in the past.

I was looking for my type. Young, slender, with a pretty face and sadness in her eyes. The sort that Evangeline Grant had been, that Robin had been, and that many others whose names I never knew, whom I sometimes remembered and sometimes forgot, had also been.

I wanted conversation, and help, and I was walking the blocks looking for a bedmate.

She was standing in the entrance to a darkened movie theater on Seventh between Forty-sixth and Forty-seventh. She was a little shorter than medium height, slender, darkhaired. She wore a tight black skirt and a pale blue blouse. Her shoes were low heeled and badly scuffed. She had a black leather purse in her hand and a raincoat over one arm. She was smoking a filter cigarette.

I said, "Nice night."

"Uh-huh. But a little cold."

"You ought to put that coat on."

"I know, but I hate the way I look in it." Her eyes reached for mine, caught hold. "What time is it?"

"I don't know. I think around three-thirty."

"Pretty late."

"Uh-huh."

I lit a cigarette. I shifted stupidly from one foot to the other. I said, the words oddly spaced, "Do you want to go out?"

"Sure."

"Okay."

She tossed her own cigarette aside. "How much will you give me?"

I shrugged.

"Will you give me twenty?"

"All right."

Her face, small and birdlike, suddenly lost its tension and relaxed into a quick smile. She moved forward from the shadows and took my arm. She asked if I had a room we could go to. I said that I didn't. Wasn't I staying at a hotel? I said I was staying with a friend.

"There's a hotel a few blocks from here where they know me," she said. "We shouldn't have any trouble getting in. The night man knows me. You mind walking a couple blocks?"

I had a sinking feeling that she was going to lead me to the Maxfield. I asked where the hotel was.

"Forty-fifth Street."

The Maxfield was on Forty-ninth. I said it was okay, and we crossed Seventh and Broadway and headed downtown. We turned the corner of Forty-fifth Street and she made me wait in a doorway to make sure we were not being followed. I waited while she returned to the corner and checked. She was visibly relaxed again when she returned to me.

"If there are any police back there," she said, "then they're invisible. What's your name?"

"Doug."

"Mine's Jackie."

"Like Jackie Kennedy?"

"Yeah." She squeezed my hand. "Jacqueline," she said. "You figure she'll sue me for having the same name?"

"I don't think so."

"People get on your back for all kinds of reasons. Like when I had to check for police, that they might be following us. I didn't mean to leave you standing there like that."

"Oh, that's all right."

"But it has been very warm here lately. A lot of arrests, you know. Ever since the killing."

The angel had brought it up herself. "I read about it."

"It's a scary thing. You never know who you're going with, you just go and hope it'll be a nice guy. Like you seem like a nice guy to me. I like uniforms."

"Even on cops?"

She laughed, delighted. "Except on cops," she said. "What are you in, Doug, the Army or the Air Force?"

"Army."

"I suppose I should be able to tell, but I don't know the difference in the uniform. Were you overseas?"

I made up some fort that I was stationed at. I don't remember it. She asked something else, and I passed the question and asked her if she had known Robin Canelli.

"I knew Robin very well," she said.

"Were you out that night?"

"Yeah." She sighed, and squeezed my arm tighter. "It's just across Eighth Avenue on the right. You see it? Hotel Claypool."

"I see it."

At the corner she said, "Yeah, I was out that very night. It was Saturday night, I was out. It could of been me. The next few days after I heard what happened I couldn't eat, I couldn't go out, nothing. All I could think of was it could of been me. You just never know what you're getting."

"Uh-huh."

"And, you know, you're all alone in the room with a man, and what are you going to do? I never had anybody like that. Of course I didn't, otherwise I wouldn't be here. But some strange men. A lot of them who want to slap a person around and other things like that. Strange. I wonder what makes a person that way?"

The desk clerk at the Claypool looked like that actor who always plays the terrified bank teller in holdup movies. His eyes bulged behind huge glasses. I gave him $5.25 for the room and the tax and signed the card *Major & Mrs. Douglas MacEwan.* He gave me the key and left us to find the room on our own.

It was a flight up. There was an elevator but we took the stairs. The room was small, with a bed and a dresser and a sink and a chair, nothing else. A card on the dresser advised that television sets were available. I wondered if anybody ever wanted one.

"It's a clean place," Jackie said. It did seem better than most of the hooker hotels. She switched on the overhead light, a dangling bare bulb, and closed and latched the door. She turned to me, and I looked at her face and tried to guess how old she might be. She had old eyes, and the skin around them was drawn and sallow, but her mouth looked young and her face unlined. Late twenties, early thirties.

"I'll have to ask you for the twenty dollars now," she said.

I found a twenty dollar bill and gave it to her. I was running low on money. The sailors and Doug had provided me with operating capital, but it wouldn't last forever. At twenty dollars an interview, I wouldn't be able to ask very many whores what they knew about Robin Canelli.

"Thank you," she said.

She put the bill in her purse, put the purse on the chair, draped the raincoat over the purse, and turned to smile at me. Her fingers, trained by frequent practice, worked the buttons of her blouse. "You can get undressed now, honey."

I sat down on the bed and took a lot of time unlacing my shoes. I kept a careful eye on her to make sure she was undressing. Sometimes a hooker will wait until a John is undressed, then bolt with his money, figuring he can't chase her without any clothes on. But she was playing the game honestly. She took off blouse and bra and skirt. She was not wearing a slip, just a pair of white nylon panties, torn on the side. She took these off, too, and I looked at her.

Very slender. Thin in the wrists and ankles. Fragile. A good trim bottom, and breasts that were small but nicely shaped and firm. Economical breasts, an economical body. All things in moderation, nothing to excess.

I wanted her.

Which was absurd, but undeniable. I had both shoes off now. She leaned against the dresser, lit a cigarette, watched me patiently.

I said, "I don't suppose you actually saw this Robin girl get picked up by the killer, did you?"

"Why?"

"I just wondered."

"To tell you the truth, I don't even like to think about it. It gives me the shakes."

"I can imagine. Then you did see him?"

"Who?"

"The killer."

"No, I didn't. I think I was with somebody at the time."

"Oh."

She moved closer to me. I was on my feet now, unbuttoning my shirt. I suppose in the army they call it a blouse or a tunic. I was unbuttoning my shirt, and trying not to notice the closeness of her, the pale skin, the needle marks on the upper arms.

"The way you talk, you sound more interested in Robin than me."

"Oh, I was just interested."

"Uh-huh. Aren't you gonna take your hat off?"

She reached out a hand, took off the dress cap. I started to smile, and then I saw the change in her eyes and my own smile died. She took a step backward, looked at me, looked past me at the closed door.

I said, "Take it easy, Jackie."

"You're him."

"Jackie—"

"Oh Jesus God."

"I'm not going to—"

"You cut your hair but it's you. Oh Jesus God in Heaven. Oh my God."

One hand was at her side, the other at her throat, as if to ward off the knife I did not have. Her face was absolutely bloodless. I have never seen anyone so profoundly naked.

"I won't hurt you."

If she heard me she gave no sign of it. She stood, quite frozen, and then after a moment her little hand fell in slow motion from her throat to her side. She drew a deep breath and closed her eyes.

She said, "You want to kill me, do it now. I could stand it now, I don't care, I'm not afraid. You want to kill me, do it now."

· 17 ·

I GOT HER PURSE FROM THE CHAIR, OPENED IT, TOOK OUT MY twenty. She watched without a word as I did this. I closed the purse and put it down on the chair. I got onto the bed and moved over against the wall to leave her access to the door. She looked at the chair and at the door and at me.

"Jackie."

She waited.

"You can put your clothes on. I won't touch you. You can get dressed, and if you want you can leave. Or you can get dressed and sit down and let me talk for a few minutes, and if you do that you can have the twenty dollars back. Either way you walk out of here. I'm not a killer."

"You say."

"I never killed anyone."

"I know you're him. I got eyes."

"I'm Alex Penn, yes."

"First that other girl, and then Robin—"

"I never hurt either of them."

"You say."

I pointed to the chair. "First get your clothes on. Then you can decide whether or not you want the twenty dollars. If you'd rather leave, you don't even have to run. You can walk out."

"I don't—"

"Get dressed."

She went over to the chair and began dressing. I ignored her and put my shoes on again and rebuttoned my shirt. She dressed even more speedily and economically than she undressed. When she finished she turned to me. She looked as though she was hunting for words.

I got out the twenty and handed it to her. She shook her head and took a step backward. I shrugged and set the twenty down on top of the bed.

"You keep the money," she said.

"Suit yourself."

"I don't want it now." She got a cigarette but couldn't get the match lit. I got to my feet and scratched a match for her. She was afraid to come to me for the light, and I saw her fear and smiled at it, and that put her a little at ease. She drew deeply on the cigarette, let the smoke out in a sigh.

"You want to talk about something."

"That's right."

"That's what you picked me up for, to talk. About Robin."

"Right."

She thought about this. "You didn't kill Robin."

"No."

"Or anybody else, that's what you said, Doug. Oh, look at that, I called you Doug. Not that I ever figured it was your name. I don't suppose anybody gives his straight name to a girl. But you need something to call a person, don't you?"

"Sure."

"What do I call you? Alexander?"

"Just Alex."

"Alex. I like that. Alex." She savored the name, then abruptly remembered what we were here for. "If you didn't kill Robin," she said, "then who did?"

"That's what I'm trying to find out."

"But you went out with her that night, didn't you? To the Maxfield?"

I gave her a capsule version of what had happened that

night and the following morning. I told her briefly how memory had returned, how I knew with complete assurance that another hand had wielded the knife and left me to take the blame. She listened to every word and her eyes never left my face.

When I ran out of words we stood there in that little room and looked at each other for a long time.

Until finally she said, "You want to know something crazy? I believe you."

No one had said that before.

We caught a taxi on Eighth Avenue. She had said that we couldn't stay in the hotel, that it was not safe. "I have a place uptown that's safe. God, I must be crazy. I have an apartment on Eighty-ninth Street, I never take anyone there." So we left the hotel and took a cab, and in it I sat so that the driver could not catch my face in his mirror. She gave him the address, and he read us as a soldier and a whore on the way to a bed, and we sat in stony silence until the cab dropped us on Eighty-ninth Street between Columbus and Amsterdam.

When he pulled away, properly paid and tipped, she took my arm. "It's a block from here, toward the park. In case he remembers your face later, this way he won't know the address."

I hadn't thought of that.

We walked to her building, a brownstone in a row of brownstones. Her apartment was on the third floor. We climbed stairs, and she opened the door with a key. When we were inside she locked the door and set the police lock, a steel bar set into a plate on the floor and angled against the door.

"I don't drink, so I don't keep anything around. I could make some coffee."

"Oh, don't bother."

"Sure, I'll make us both some coffee. Sit down, I'll make the coffee."

She went into the kitchen and I heard water running. I

wandered around the living room. The furniture was old and the rug worn, but the pieces were comfortable together. I walked to the window. It faced out on a blank wall, an air shaft, but I pulled the shade anyway.

"The water's up," she said. "I only have instant, I hope it's all right."

"Instant is fine."

"Cream and sugar?"

"Just black is fine."

"You're like me, but I always put in an icecube so it cools faster. You want an icecube?"

"I'll try it."

We settled down on the couch with cups of black coffee. She curled her thin legs under her, and I caught an instant of *déjà vu*. It took a minute to identify it, and then I remembered how Linda had curled herself into the identical position two nights back.

She said, "I've been here almost three years. I never brought anyone here before. Not even when it's been very warm and the hotels just won't let anybody in, not even girls they know well. I would always find a hotel in some other neighborhood where I could get in, maybe Twenty-third Street. Or I would just not work that night, but I would never bring a trick here, not once."

"I appreciate it."

"But you're not safe around Times Square, you know. I think the uniform is a very good idea, but even so someone is gonna recognize you sooner or later. Here, nobody knows you're here. Except me."

I lit us each a cigarette.

"Cause once the cops get you, you're dead."

"I know it."

"I wish I could say that I saw something, like somebody following you and Robin to the Maxfield. But I didn't even see you pick her up. I was with somebody."

"You told me."

"Well, at the time I would of told you that anyway. Not to get involved, you understand?" She sipped her coffee. "Do you have any idea who did it? Any suspects?"

"Nothing much."

"Tell me."

So I did. I gave her the unabridged edition this time, all of it, front to back. She was the first person to hear the whole thing, and it did me good to tell it. She was just the right kind of sounding board. She stayed with every word, nodding to show that she was following me, interrupting now and then when she wanted a point cleared up. Linda disgusted her, MacEwan appalled her, and the problem of finding out who did what appeared to intrigue her.

She didn't think much of my idea of picking up a girl and asking her questions. "No one would tell you anything," she said. "They'd just run."

"You didn't run."

"Well, I told you I was crazy." She considered that. "What happened was I decided to trust you."

"I trust you, too."

"What's to trust? What could I do to you?"

"Call the police."

"Me?" She laughed. "The police and I"—holding up two fingers pressed together—"are not exactly like this."

"Even so."

"I hate to tell you this, I'm not proud of it, but I've been arrested. I've been in jail. Not just once. A few times."

"That must be rough."

"Rough! You know the House of Detention? In the Village?"

"I know where it is."

She turned her eyes away. "I shouldn't mention it. You can't think much of me."

"I was inside just once, but for a lot longer than you."

"It's different."

"Maybe in some ways. I think I understand you better than

you think, Jackie. You don't have to worry about what you say to me."

Long silence. Then, "There's worse."

"Oh?"

"Well, you probably know it already. One of the reasons I couldn't stay at the hotel forever, I had to come back here."

During the past few minutes her eyes had been running, and she had been sniffing nervously. I knew what was coming.

"You saw my arms."

"Sure."

"Well, then, you know."

"Sure. You use stuff."

"Yeah."

"So?"

A longer silence this time. Then, "I have to fix now. I don't want you to see me. It would make you sick."

"No, it wouldn't."

"I don't mean sick, I mean you wouldn't like me, seeing it. I want to go in the other room."

"All right."

"Alex?"

"What?"

"I'll just be a minute."

"All right."

"You'll stay here? You won't leave? Because I think maybe I can help you. I mean finding out who did it. You won't go?"

"Where would I go?"

"I don't know. Away, I guess."

"I won't go anywhere."

"Good." She was rubbing at her eyes with the back of her hand. She got to her feet and walked quickly out of the room. "I'll be right back, Alex. I won't be more than a minute, I'll be right back."

· 18 ·

THE CHANGE WAS INSTANTLY VISIBLE WHEN SHE RETURNED. IT was much more than a matter of pupil dilation. Her face, nervous and animated before she fixed, was now profoundly relaxed. She walked slowly, as if with cushioned feet, and her shoulders drooped. She sat on the couch, her feet out in front of her, and said, "Too bright, too bright," and I went around turning off lights.

After awhile she said, "I was off for a whole year. I wasn't working. There was this man. He lived in Scarsdale. Do you know where that is?"

"Yes."

"I was never there. Is it nice?"

"Yes."

"He was married. He paid for my apartment and gave me money, and I didn't see anybody else. I saw him during the day, or sometimes he would stay over." She closed her eyes. Her cigarette burned down, and I took it from between her fingers and put it out. Then she opened her eyes and looked at me. "I was in love with him," she said.

Her voice was very soft and she spoke slowly, levelly. Only her lips moved. Before she had talked with her hands, but now they remained still in her lap.

"An hour here, an hour there. And during the summer he always took his wife to Europe for two months. He would send the children to a camp in New England and take his wife to

Europe, every summer. So this one summer, when we were seeing each other, he was going to give me a trip. He would let me buy a new wardrobe and he would arrange a trip for me to Puerto Rico. He would take care of the hotel and the airplane ticket and everything, you know?"

"Uh-huh."

"And I was very excited about this. Are you from New York, Alex?"

"No."

"Where?"

"Ohio."

"Is it nice there?"

"Not especially."

"Oh. But I'm from New York, see, and I was never anyplace. Always here in New York. So I was very excited about the trip, and I started shopping for clothes, and then this man explained to me that his business was bad and he couldn't afford to pay for the trip. He could give me some money, but not enough for the trip." The eyes closed again. I smoked half a cigarette, and then, eyes still shut, she said, "He could still send his kids to that camp and take his wife to Europe, but he couldn't afford the trip for me. See?"

"I see."

"So I was very hurt, Alex, and when he came back from Europe I didn't live there any more. I started working again, tricking, and I started using stuff again, and I stopped being in love with him, and when he came back I didn't live there any more."

She fell silent again. I looked at her and wanted to touch her face.

She said, "Everybody needs a crutch, that's all. Everybody has his own hang-up." She opened her eyes. "Here I'm telling you things I don't ever tell anybody. Alex? How come you picked me up?"

"I wanted to find out if—"

"No no no. I saw you on the street, you know, back and

forth, back and forth. There were a lot of girls out tonight. What made you pick me?"

"You were the prettiest."

She opened her eyes very wide and turned a little toward me. Truth is perhaps contagious; I had not meant to tell her that, had tried to avoid telling it to myself, but it had come out. She studied my eyes very closely.

"You're a very nice person, Alex."

I looked at her and didn't know what to do.

"Yes," she said, very softly, to the question I had not asked. "I would like it very much, Alex."

So I kissed her.

She kissed greedily, eagerly, like a yearning schoolgirl in a parked car. She kissed warm and wet and tightened her arms around my neck. She kissed sweet and soft, and I rubbed the back of her neck and stroked her like a frightened kitten.

We walked drunkenly to her little bedroom and stopped to kiss in the doorway. She sighed, and murmured my name. We entered the bedroom and left the lights out. We undressed. She drew down the bedclothing and we lay down on the bed together.

"Well, it took awhile, but here we are. Who would of guessed?"

"Shhhh."

"Alex—"

We kissed, and she clung to me, and I felt the awesome softness of her. Every bit of her was soft and smooth. I could not stop touching her. I touched her breasts, her belly, her back, her bottom, her legs. I loved the way she felt.

She lay quite still, eyes closed, body at peace, in the sweet inertia of heroin, while I wrote song lyrics on all the delights of her flesh. I stroked her and kissed her, and at length her body began to make sweet abbreviated movements, and her breathing matched these movements in rhythm. She made small noises, sweet dim sounds. I ceased to think, I lost myself utterly in the smell taste touch of her. And at length she said, suddenly urgent, "Now, darling, now."

I threw myself down upon that small soft body, and her hand clutched me and tucked me home. She worked and strained in sweet agony beneath me. I brought her there. I heard her cry out and felt her quiver, and then I melted at last inside her in unutterable delight.

She came back from the bathroom. I had not moved or opened my eyes. She slipped into bed beside me and said, "I'm not sick, you don't have to worry."

"I wasn't worried."

"You must of been."

"No."

"I had the clap three times. The other, never." Her voice was flat. "I been everything, I had everything. I wish to hell I was somebody else."

"I don't."

"I'll wake up and you'll be gone."

"No."

"In your little soldier suit."

"No."

"Hold onto me, Alex, I feel all shaky."

She was small and soft in my arms. I kissed her. She opened her eyes for a moment, then closed them again and relaxed. I let my own eyes slip shut and discovered how exhausted I was. There was a curtain ready to come down and I wasn't going to fight it.

She said, "The watch and the wallet. And Robin's purse."

"Huh?"

"Tomorrow."

"I don't follow you."

She spoke with an effort, dragging the words up one by one. "The man who killed them. I just had an idea. Tomorrow. First sleep."

We fell asleep holding each other.

· 19 ·

When I awoke a little before noon Jackie brought me a cup of coffee and a sweet roll. "I usually eat breakfast around the corner," she said. "But I figured the less you go out and let people see you, the better. The roll okay?"

"Fine."

"I bought you some socks and underwear. I hope everything's the right size. It's just schlock from Columbus Avenue but at least it's clean."

I got dressed. The socks and underwear were the right size. I felt a little foolish putting on my uniform again, but it still seemed a worthwhile disguise. I went into the kitchen and got another cup of coffee and took it into the living room.

We smoked and drank coffee. She had evidently fixed an hour or so before, as well as I could judge. Her movements were slow and studied, but she wasn't as obviously junked up as she had been the night before. Her face, clean and fresh, looked very vulnerable. She would dart quick looks at me, then turn her attention back to cigarette and coffee.

After a while I said, "Well, I guess I better get going."

"Who said?"

"Well, I—"

She turned away. "Go, if you want to. You don't have to stay on my account."

I put out my cigarette and set the empty cup on the coffee table, but I stayed on the couch. I hadn't seen the script yet and I didn't know my lines. She was a hooker and I was a John, she was an angel of mercy and I was a man in trouble, she was Jane and I was Tarzan, all those things. I didn't know my lines.

Without looking at me she said, "You don't remember what I said last night? About the watch and the wallet and the purse?"

I had forgotten.

"Because that part of it doesn't add up right," she said. "I thought if we sort of picked at it we might get somewheres. See what I mean?"

"I don't think so."

"Well, Alex, what I mean is, what happened to your watch and wallet?"

"They must have been stolen."

"And Robin's purse?"

"I didn't know she had one."

"She always carried a purse. Same as I always do. I make sure I get the money as soon as I'm in the room with the fellow, and I put my coat or something over the purse. You know, on a chair or on the dresser. I know Robin always did the same."

I closed my eyes, trying to remember. It was getting increasingly harder to bring that particular night back into focus. It seemed to me now that I remembered a purse, that she had taken my money and tucked it into a purse, but I couldn't be entirely sure.

"Maybe she had a purse. I don't know."

"She must of had one, Alex. A lot of the colored girls don't, they like to leave their bras on and they'll tuck the bills in there, but most men don't like that. Leaving the bra on, I mean."

"Uh-huh."

"Anyway, she had to have a purse. And you had your watch and wallet, didn't you?"

"I hardly thought about it. I just supposed that they had been stolen somewhere along the line."

"But you had them when you went with Robin."

"Did I?"

She spread her small hands. "Well, what else? You paid Robin, didn't you? You gave her some money?"

"Twenty dollars."

"You must of given her money if you made love to her. So that means you had the watch and wallet when you went with her."

"I guess so." I looked at her, the small intense eyes, the head tilted forward in concentration. "But what difference does it make? If I had them then, I certainly didn't have them when I woke up the next morning. So—"

"Well, what happened to them?"

"Oh."

"You see what I mean, Alex?"

"I never even thought of it."

"Well, see, you were too busy concentrating on who could of done it, and then you didn't stop to think about just what it was that happened. But that was one of the first things I thought of, that the watch and the wallet were gone. And Robin's purse, too. It wasn't there when you woke up?"

"If it was, I never saw it."

"Would you of noticed it?"

"I'm not sure. But the watch and the wallet were gone. Unless they were in the purse."

"You mean if Robin took them?" I nodded. "No," she said, shaking her head emphatically. "Robin didn't take them. Robin never stole."

"Never?"

"No. Neither do I, I never steal. I did once, a long time ago. A man who passed out. We didn't even make love, he just got on the bed and passed out. And I went through his wallet and took his money. Not his wallet, but just the money from it. Almost a hundred dollars. I felt bad about it. I don't mean I sat around crying, but I felt bad about it."

She fell silent, her gaze turned inward, fastening upon the memory and the way she had felt. "I never did it again," she said. "A lot of the girls do, maybe most of them, but I never do, and neither did Robin. I'm pretty sure of that."

"Then the watch and wallet—"

"Maybe the killer."

"But why?"

A shrug. "Everybody likes money."

"Not the man who framed me. I didn't have much in the wallet, and the watch wasn't worth a fortune. And whoever set me up for this wouldn't take chances for a few dollars. It doesn't make sense."

"Suppose he hired someone."

I had briefly considered this possibility, but I had not wanted to dwell on it. Because once I allowed it, my elimination process went utterly out the window. The proof that Russell Stone, for example, was not in New York Saturday night—it counted for nothing once I admitted that he could have hired someone to do his killing for him. Still, like it or not, it was quite possible. And it was similarly possible that a hired killer would take the trouble to add a watch and wallet and a whore's purse to his haul.

"We can forget the purse and the wallet," she was saying. "Whoever he was, he'd just take the money and ditch the rest. Stick them in a trashcan, probably. That's no help."

"What about the watch?"

"That's our chance." Her teeth worried her lower lip. "I hope it wasn't a really cheap watch. Like they sell in drugstores for $10.95."

"It was worth about a hundred new. Maybe a little more."

"Well, that's one for our side. You know the make?"

"Elgin. It said *Lord Elgin* on the dial."

"You would know it if you saw it?"

"I suppose so." I concentrated. "There was a link missing in the band, and—"

"Forget the band. It probably has a new band by now."

"Oh. Just a minute. I think I could recognize it by the face. There's a nick in the paint around the dial. If I saw it, I'm sure I would know it. But why? How could we find it?"

"If he stole it to keep it, then we can't. Unless you walk around the city until you happen to see it on somebody's wrist. But if he stole it to sell it, it's less than a week, and whoever took it probably still has it. A watch that's worth around a hundred dollars, you could fence it almost anywhere. I mean you wouldn't have to go to an important fence. Just any pawnshop, and you would get ten or fifteen dollars for it. Maybe twenty, but probably ten or fifteen. So if we go looking to buy a watch, and we happen to see it—"

"It sounds impossible, Jackie."

"You think so?"

"You said it yourself. How many pawnshops are there in the city? And how many watches? It could be anywhere."

"It's most likely around midtown. There's some places a person would be most likely to go."

"Still—"

"Can you think of a better place to start?"

"No, but—"

"I know a few people in hockshops." Her hand moved, unconsciously, I think, to her upper arm. A sweater covered the hit marks, but I had seen them last night. "The scene I have, things of mine go in and out of hockshops. So there's some people I know."

She was right. It was a place to start. "We'll try it," I said.

"Let me get a coat on."

"All right."

At the doorway I said, "Jackie, why are you doing this? Why take the trouble?"

"What's it matter?"

"I just wondered."

She shrugged but didn't say anything. The sun was bright outside, and she took sunglasses from her purse and put them on. We walked toward the park to catch a taxi. While we were waiting she said, "You want to know something? I like you, Alex. I don't like many people. That I can talk to and relax with."

I found her hand. It was small and soft, and cold.

"Do you like me, Alex?"

"Yes."

"Don't say it unless it's true."

"I like you, Jackie."

"You ought to pull your cap down a little. You don't want too much of your face showing."

"All they notice is the uniform."

"I suppose."

"You're a sweet person, Jackie."

We stood waiting. There was a dearth of empty cabs. I lit us each a cigarette. She said, "Look, don't make me a saint. Maybe I'm just interested, you know? Nothing ever happens. Something to do, you know?"

"Sure."

She was superb in the pawnshops. Before we went to the first place, on Eighth Avenue just below Forty-seventh Street, she went over the routine with me. "Now the way it ought to play is that I'm in love with you and I want to buy you a present. See, the places we'll be going, they'll know that I'm a prostitute. So what they'll figure is that you're my man, and they'll think, you know, a prostitute and her man, and they won't be afraid to show a watch that is hot, like they might be otherwise."

Prostitute. The word had an odd sound on her lips. Unlike the slang and the euphemisms, it was clinically accurate, devoid of the usual overtones. *A prostitute and her man.*

We played it by ear at the first shop and refined the script as we went along. First we would stand around outside, studying the watches on display in the window. Then, inside, she would explain that we wanted to buy a watch. A decent watch, and it had to have a sweep second hand—mine had

had one, and that was one quick way to narrow down the entries.

"What was the brand you said you liked, honey?"

"Lord Elgin."

"That's it. Do you have any Lord Elgins?"

They usually did; it's not an uncommon watch. And they showed us tray after tray of watches. We made a great business of looking at watches, with Jackie now and then pointing one out and asking me if I didn't like it, and with me always finding some reason to reject what was shown to me. We were careful to seem like live customers. If the pawnbroker had a Lord Elgin in stock, we wanted to make damned certain we got a look at it.

And we went from shop to shop, and looked at watch after watch after watch, and kept not finding mine.

We broke for a late lunch, bacon and eggs at an Automat on Sixth Avenue. I said, "Well, it was a good idea."

"We'll find it, Alex."

"I don't even know if I would recognize the damned thing. I've seen so many watches already today. Maybe somebody showed it to me and I didn't spot it."

"You would know it. How long have you had it?"

"I don't know. Eight, ten years. Gwen gave it to me."

"Your wife?"

"That's right."

"Oh." She took a sip of coffee. "If you wore it all that time, you'll know it when you see it. And there are more places to try. We'll find the watch."

"Maybe."

"You don't like what we're pretending, do you?"

"I don't understand."

"You know. That you're my man."

"I don't mind."

"No?" She searched my eyes, then looked away. "I don't blame you," she said.

"I really don't mind it."

"It doesn't matter."

I wanted to change the subject. "Did Robin have a man?"

"Why?"

"I don't know. If she did, he might know something."

"She had somebody. Danny, his name was. But he died about, oh, two or three weeks before she did. Two weeks, I think. An OD. That's an overdose. Heroin."

"He used it, too?"

"Oh, sure. And Robin had to hustle twice as hard. Two habits, you know. Anybody who says two can live as cheap as one isn't on stuff." She shifted in her seat. "I'm getting a little ginchy, like I should go back to the apartment and fix. It's not time. I think it's talking about it that's doing it. Sometimes it's in the mind, you know? How did we get on this subject?"

"Robin's man."

"Yeah. I don't know. He got a cap that wasn't cut the way they usually are, or he used two caps to get up higher, or something. He died with a needle in his arm and Robin was there when it happened. Oh, Jesus. I don't want to talk about it any more."

"All right."

"Let's get out of here."

"You want to go back to the apartment, Jackie?"

"No, I'm all right."

"You sure?"

"I'm all right. It's my hangup and I know what it's all about." She took my arm. "We'll find your watch," she said. "I got a feeling."

And we did, three or four places later, three or four blocks downtown and a block west. In a secondhand shop with a window full of radios and cameras and typewriters, we looked at a few watches, and then Jackie asked me what brand it was that I was especially interested in, and I said Lord Elgin right on cue, and the little old man in shirtsleeves remembered a Lord Elgin in truly perfect shape, a bargain, he could give us an awfully good price on it, and it was my watch he showed me.

He'd changed the band, just as Jackie had said he would. But it was the same watch and I would have known it a block off. "This is it," I said. And added, "This is just what we've been looking for."

Jackie reached to take it from me, nudging me with her foot. I guessed that this meant I should shut up and follow her lead. She studied the watch, then asked the price.

"Forty-five dollars."

She thought it over, then set it down on the counter. "We'll think it over," she said. "We'll be back."

"Forty dollars," the man suggested.

"We just want to go outside and talk it over in private."

"At forty it's a bargain. I bought it reasonable myself, that's why I can offer it to you so cheap. You know what these cost new?"

"We just want to talk," she said, and we got out of there.

We walked to the corner. She said, "You're sure that's the one, Alex? Because you have to be sure."

"I'm positive. I'd know it anywhere."

"Good. I knew we'd find it sooner or later, I had a feeling. Now we got to figure out how to find out where he got it. Let me think a minute."

I lit a cigarette. The excitement was beginning to bubble inside me. I wanted to go back to the store and grab the little man by the throat. "I'll shake it out of him," I said.

"No."

"He'll tell us. Why not?"

"No. Wait a minute."

I waited.

"If it weren't for the damned uniform you could pretend to be a cop," she said. "But that's no good now. What do they call them—Army Police?"

"Military Police. MP's."

"Yeah. Could you be something like that? But not after the bit we been working, it wouldn't go down right. Let me think. Do you have about fifty dollars?"

"I think so."

"Make sure."

I checked my roll. I had seventy dollars and change. "It won't leave much," I said, "but I've got it."

"Good."

"Why fifty? He said forty."

"Forty for the watch. Ten more for him to remember where he got it. We got to scare him and bribe him both. C'mon."

We went back into the store. He seemed surprised to see us. He had already put the watch away. He got it out, and I handed him forty dollars in fives and tens.

"I'll have to charge you the tax—"

"No tax," Jackie said.

"Listen, I don't make the rules."

"You make the prices. You'd of taken thirty-five and we both know it. You absorb the tax."

"Well, I suppose I could do that—"

"And while you're at it," she said, watch in hand, "You can tell us who laid the watch on you, baby."

He just looked at her.

"It was boosted Saturday night," she went on. There was a tough, flat quality to her voice that I had not heard before. "Somebody brought it here Monday morning. You tell me who."

"Now, miss, you must be thinking of some other watch. I've had this particular watch in stock for over three months, and—"

She was shaking her head. "No."

"A lot of watches look alike. Lord Elgin, that's not an uncommon—"

"No."

He didn't say anything. He had the money and we had the watch, and it was our move, and he didn't get it.

She said, "You got the forty, that's what you paid plus a profit. All we want is a name."

"Believe me, if I could help you—"

"You'd rather talk to the cops?"

The round face turned sly. "I have a feeling," he said, "that if you wanted to go to the police, you wouldn't pay me forty dollars. The interest you have in this, you don't want police."

"Maybe."

"So?"

"So it's a private matter."

"Everything's a private matter. Nothing you come across these days is anything but a private matter."

Scratch a receiver of stolen goods and you find a philosopher. I said, "All right, so tell him."

Jackie looked at me, puzzled.

"We were at a private party Saturday night," I said. "That's when the watch was taken. So you can see what that means. It was taken by someone at the party, and everyone there was a friend of ours. At least we thought so."

"Ah," the man said.

She came in on cue. "Which means we do not want police."

"This I can understand."

"But," I said, "we would also like to know who our friends are."

"So who wouldn't like to know this?"

"Uh-huh."

A sigh. "If I could help you."

"Just a name."

"I could tell you a name, and it wouldn't mean anything, and I could say that this is the only name I know, and then what?"

"And a description."

"So what's a description? It might fit someone and it might not, and the person who took the watch, if this was the watch you lost, might not be the same person who sold it to me. If this was the watch in question."

Jackie looked at him, then at the watch. She handed the watch to me and I put it on. I liked the old band better. I asked him if he had the old band around, and he looked at me for a moment and then smiled. He seemed to be enjoying this.

Jackie said, "If you don't give us a name and a description, or if you do and we don't get anywhere with it, somebody else is going to come here and ask the same questions, and it might be somebody who isn't as nice as us."

"Such threats from such a nice couple."

"Sometimes threats come true."

"Like wishes?"

We fenced like this, the three of us, with Jackie carrying most of the load while I picked up a cue now and then and helped her along. She was getting increasingly nervous, and several times I saw her rub the back of her hand over her nose or mouth. Her eyes were watering behind the dark glasses. A rage mounted in me, and I wanted to grab the round little man and hurt him.

The rage passed, but I reached out mental fingers and pulled it back for another look at it. And I took out another ten dollar bill and put it down on the counter, and he looked at it and at me.

I said, "That's ten more dollars for a name and a description. You better take it, and you better deliver."

"And if it's a lie that I sell you?"

"Then I come back here," I said, "and I kill you."

"Would you really do this?"

"Is it worth finding out?"

He decided it wasn't.

THE ONLY NAME I HAVE FOR HIM IS PHIL. IT COULD BE HIS
*name. Who knows? Age, I would say, late twenties. I think he
is Italian. Maybe Jewish, but I would think Italian. On the
short side. Maybe five-foot-seven. A little shorter than myself,
I would say. Dark hair, black, not too long and not too short.
No part, just combed straight back. A pointed face like a
piece of pie, you know what I mean? Like a triangle. Long
nose. Thin lips. Pockmarks on his cheeks and chin. Walks with
his shoulders hunched forward. Thin in the body. Very nervous, with the hands moving all the time. . . .*

When we'd been over it three times, when we had all he
had to give us, I told him he should forget he ever saw us.
"You shouldn't worry," he said. "You were never here, I never
met you, you shouldn't worry."

We left the store, walked two blocks, turned a corner, stood
waiting for a cab. Jackie was overdue now. She said, "Oh,
Jesus, we got to get home. We got to get home. Is it cold out,
Alex?"

"Not very."

"I'm shivering. See how I'm shaking? He gave it to us
straight, though. He didn't want to, but he gave it to us
straight."

"Like you said, we bribed him and we scared him." She
shook visibly again, and I put an arm around her to steady
her. "You think he'll tell Phil?"

"Are you kidding? Not a chance."

"Why not?"

A cab drew up. She said, "Later," and we got in. She gave the driver the same false address half a block from her building. I sat back and she shrank against me. I put an arm around her and drew her close. She buried her face against my chest. She was shaking, and I held her tight and tried to steady her. Her whole body kept tightening up, then relaxing, then going tight again.

It was a long ride in bad traffic. From time to time she would get hold of herself and it was better, but then the shaking and twitching would come back worse than before. She was a wreck by the time we got out of the cab. I tried to talk to her on the way to her building but she was incapable of speech. She held onto my hand and hurried me along.

Inside her apartment, she said again, "You don't want to see this," and disappeared into the bedroom. I walked around the living room until she came back. I thought about what it was like to need something more than any person should need anything. A drink, or a woman. I thought first that those needs were different, that they didn't make one shake that much or sweat that way. Then I decided that they were the same after all, that one hangup is the same as another, that the shakes were always there.

When she came into the living room she told me that she wished she was dead. I told her to cut it out. She said she meant it. I kissed her, and she started to cry, and I held onto her and kissed her until she stopped.

I left her sitting on the couch, eyes closed, while I made us some coffee. When I sat down next to her I asked her how she knew the man would not tip off Phil.

"The same reason he finally told you. He's scared."

"That I'll come back and kill him? I think I meant it when I said it, but—"

"Not that. You didn't see his face."

"I thought I did."

"Then you didn't read it right. When you said that to him he was looking right at you, at your face, and that's when he got it. He recognized you, Alex. He knows who you are."

"Oh, no—"

"I should of thought of it right away. Maybe I would of been afraid of it. The one thing he doesn't want is to get involved in a murder. That would put him up tight all around, he couldn't stand it. So all he can do is put you onto Phil and hope the two of you kill each other or something and that it doesn't ever get back to him."

"He won't call the police?"

"Never."

"He could call anonymously. Tell them I'm wearing an army uniform, something like that."

She shook her head. "He wants you to get away for now. If you get picked up now, he knows you're going to talk about that watch. All he wants is to keep out of it." She sighed heavily. "I don't think he would ever of told us otherwise. You want to know something, baby? People are just too much. When he thought we were just a couple of people who got robbed he wouldn't even tell us what time it was. But as soon as you're a murderer, then he wants to give us his right arm on a silver dish. People are beautiful."

"Uh-huh."

"Alex? I got to fall out for a little while. I won't be asleep, just sitting. But I can't talk. You want to watch the television? Or put on some music on the radio?"

"Maybe some music."

"Something slow and quiet. I had a little more just now than I should of."

"Are you all right?"

"Uh-huh."

"You sure?"

"Ummm."

I took the cigarette from between her fingers and put it out. She sat virtually motionless for a little over an hour, now and then nodding her head slightly in time to the music. When she came up out of it she asked me for a cigarette. I lit one for her. She took two puffs on it and gave it back and asked me to put it out. I did.

She said that I must hate her. I said I loved her, and we went to bed.

· 21 ·

SHE SAID, "YOU SLEEP, BABY. I GOT TO GO OUT FOR A WHILE.
I'll be back. You just sleep."

I dozed for a few more hours. She had not returned when I
finally dragged myself out of bed. I showered, then poked
around in the medicine cabinet until I found her little electric
razor and shaved with it. I was hungry, but the cupboard was
bare. I made myself a cup of coffee and took it into the living
room.

There wasn't much to read, just a stack of paperbacks. A
couple of novels about American nurses in the Far East. Had
my Jackie wanted, in the years before needles and commercial
love, to tend the sick? To comfort the wounded? There was a
reprint of a big best seller and a few sex-fact books, including
one psychoanalytical study of a prostitute. I skimmed this last,
but I couldn't concentrate on what I was reading. The words
didn't register. I put the books back and made more coffee.

We were going to find this Phil. Someone had hired him,
and we would find out who and why, and we would wrap it
all up and hand it to the police and it would be over, all of
it.

I was very certain of this now. Before I had possessed the
knowledge of my own innocence and little more than that.
There was no place to get started, nothing but random facts
and inferences that refused to add up to anything concrete.

Jackie had changed this. Because of her, we knew who sold my watch. That gave us a handle, and we could pull the rest of it along.

She was out now, talking to people, finding out who this Phil might be.

I lit a cigarette. Once I was cleared, it would be no great problem getting a university job again. I had been a good scholar and a good teacher. They would want me back. Of course there were wasted years, and they made a difference. I had been close to a departmental chairmanship, and now it was unlikely that I would ever rise that high. I was starting fresh, in a sense, and starting at a less than tender age.

The hell, it hardly mattered. I'd have a job again, I'd do my work again, I'd be a person again.

My mind played with plans. Should I stay in New York? There was an undeniable appeal in the idea of a little college town somewhere in New England or the Midwest, a comfortable retreat away from the smell and taste of New York. But the city had things of its own going for it. It was a place to hide, a place where people let you alone.

But I didn't have to hide any more.

Of course a small town might be a better place for someone trying to shake a drug habit. I remembered having read that the worst danger for cured addicts was a return to old haunts, that this made it all too easy for old patterns to reestablish themselves. In another town, where heroin was presumably hard to find, where she didn't know the source of supply—

All of which, I told myself, was stupid sloppy romanticism. I was confusing loneliness and gratitude and mutual back-scratching with something deeper and more permanent. Stupid.

I kept getting hungrier and she kept not coming home, and after a while I wrote out a note for her and left it on top of the coffee table. I had to walk all the way over to Broadway to find an all-night diner. I had a couple of hamburgers and a plate of french fries and still more coffee. I walked back to the place. I had left the door unlatched, and it was still un-latched, and the note was on the coffee table and Jackie wasn't home yet.

It was past six by the time she unlocked the door and came in, and I had gone through a full pack of cigarettes by then. I couldn't keep from worrying. I got all the worst images—Jackie tracking down Phil, and he with a knife in his hand, and she with her hand at her throat, and the knife flashing. Jackie picked up for possession of heroin, arrested, clapped in a cell. Jackie hurt in any of a thousand idiot ways. But she came home, and I went to her and kissed her and told her I had worried about her.

"Worried?"

"You were gone so long."

"I thought you'd still be sleeping."

"No, I've been up for hours. I went out and got something to eat a little while ago. Where were you?"

"I had to find out about this Phil. You know, look around, talk to people. And then I had to work a little, you know, and I had to find a dealer and make a buy. The stuff I used before was the last of what I had around, and I had to work for awhile and then buy some more. And—"

"I had some money."

"Only twenty dollars."

"Wouldn't that have been enough?"

"I like to buy for a few days at a time. And I don't want to take money from you, Alex. I wouldn't want to do that."

"You went to bed with me and then you went out trick-ing."

"You think I wanted to?"

"You went to bed with me and then—"

Her face fell apart. She said, "Alex, you got no right, you got no goddamn right!" And ran into the bathroom and slammed the door. I heard the lock click. I went to the door and tried to tell her I was sorry. She wouldn't answer me. After a few minutes I heard the shower running, and I returned to the living room and walked around. I tried to sit down but couldn't stay still, so I got up and smoked and wore out the rug.

When she came back smelling fresh and clean and wearing a different dress, I told her again that I was sorry.

"It's all right."

"I didn't think."

"No, I was the one didn't think, Alex. I figured you would know why I went out. It was my fault for saying anything." She scooped up her purse and headed for the bedroom. I followed her. "But you can't be jealous or anything. It's not like when we make love. It's what I do, that's all. It's who I am." She turned to me. "You hate me now, don't you?"

"No."

"But you hate what I am."

"Not even that."

"Because I can't help what I am, Alex. I don't like it and I'm not proud of it but it's what I am."

The history professor's wife in the little college town, dressing the children and bundling them off to school, mingling with other wives at faculty teas, sitting up nights proofreading my books and articles. How I had miscast this girl.

"I found out about this Phil," she was saying. "That's not his name but a lot of people call him Phillie because he comes from South Philadelphia. His name is Albert Schapiro. He's not Italian, he's Jewish."

"You're sure he's the one?"

"Pretty sure. I asked around, and he sounds right."

"Is he a killer?"

"I don't know."

"But he must have killed Robin."

"I guess so." She took an envelope from her purse. "I want to stash this stuff now. Then I thought we could go find Phillie. Somebody said they heard he was staying in a hotel at Twenty-third and Tenth. You want to go?"

"Now?"

"He's probably there now. It would be a good time."

I wanted him. Oh, how I wanted him. "Let's go," I said.

That afternoon we had been a prostitute and her man. Now we were a prostitute and her client. Jackie knew the hotel, she had worked there now and then when the Times Square area was too hot, and the desk man seemed to remember her. The hotel was filthy, the lobby cluttered with winos. The desk man had a bottle of Thunderbird in an open drawer. I signed Doug MacEwan's name on the registration card and paid the man $5.75 and we headed for the stairs.

And Jackie said, "Just a minute, honey. Wait right here, something I want to ask the man."

I waited while she doubled back to the desk. I heard her ask what room Albert Schapiro was in. "Something I got to leave with him," she said. "Soon as I handle this John."

He flipped through a stack of cards and found the right one. She hurried back and joined me. "305," she said. "He gave us 214, we better go there long enough for him to forget about us."

We went to 214. It was dirtier than the Times Square hotels, and, in the light of dawn, even more depressing. I looked at the sagging bed, the sheets stained with past performance. Jackie had worked in this hotel, perhaps in this room, perhaps upon this bed. I tried not to think about this. I was not jealous. What I felt was closer to disgust, and annoyance with myself in the bargain. I told myself, hating the phrase, not to look gift whores in the mouth. I kept my eyes away from the bed and tried to concentrate on Phillie. I wondered if he would have a knife, and if he would be able to use it.

We gave the hotel ten minutes to forget us. Then she nodded shortly and opened the door, and we went back to the staircase and up a flight and found Room 305. I listened at the door and couldn't hear anything. I tried the knob. The door was locked.

Jackie knocked. There was no answer and she knocked

again, louder. A muffled voice wanted to know who the hell it was.

"Dolores."

"What is it?"

"Lemme in, it's important."

There was slow movement within the room, approaching footsteps, then the snick of a bolt being drawn back. The door eased open a few inches, and he said, "What the hell, you're not—"

I put my shoulder into the door and it flew backward, taking him with it. We went in after him. The roundfaced man had described him perfectly. There could be no mistake, he was the one. He was wearing dirty underwear, and he had needle tracks all over both arms and legs.

He looked at my uniform and he looked at Jackie and he was lost. "Whatever your thing is," he said, "you got the wrong boy. I don't get it at all."

"Albert Schapiro," I said. "Phillie."

"Yeah. So?"

"Who paid you to kill her, Phillie?"

"Kill?" His face said he didn't understand a bit of it. "I never killed nobody. Not ever."

"And you never saw the watch?"

"What are you talking about?"

I let him see the watch. He stared at it, and he did not quite manage to hide the recognition in his eyes, and then he looked at my face and saw my face instead of my uniform, and this time he didn't even try to keep it a secret. He said, "Oh, Jesus Christ, it's you," and he shoved Jackie into me and started for the door.

I got him by the arm. I yanked the arm and he spun toward me, off balance, and I let go of his arm and hit him in the face. He yelped and fell back. I grabbed the front of his undershirt with my left hand and drew him close, and I hit him in the face with my right hand. I hurt my hand but I didn't notice it. I just kept hitting him, and he went down and

I landed on top of him, and I kept on hitting him until Jackie managed to drag me away from him. My hand was bloody, I'd cut it on his teeth, and there was more blood from his broken nose. Jackie bolted the door and made me wash my hand in the sink and we waited for Phillie to wake up.

When he came to, Jackie soaked a pillowslip in the sink and cleaned up his face for him. He was in bad shape. The nose seemed to be broken, and his mouth was a mess. I had knocked two teeth out. Now, with the rage cooled, I felt oddly embarrassed by the violence.

He said, the words warped by the missing teeth, "You don't have to play so fucking rough. You coulda killed me."

"Like you killed the girl."

"I never killed nobody. You can beat me up all day long, it don't matter. I never killed nobody and I'll never say different."

"You were in the hotel room."

"I shoulda thrown that fucking watch in the river. Ten bucks and I got a broken face and more troubles. Yeah, I was in the room. By the time I got there the chick was dead and you were out cold."

"You're lying."

"The hell I am. I thought you were both dead. The first I looked, I saw the two of you, I almost fell out. I wanted to get away from there."

"Why didn't you?"

He looked at Jackie. "She's a user, isn't she? Ask her."

Jackie said, "Why were you in that hotel?"

"I was boosting, what do you think? Those hotels, they get a lot of drunks who leave their doors open. They forget to lock them. I was up tight, I was boosting. Is that a crime?"

The question was too silly to answer.

"Jesus, my nose." His fingers patted it gently. "You broke my nose."

"How did you get in the room?"

"The door was open. That goddamn watch. Ten bucks, but I never figured Solly would sing. You can't trust anybody."

I asked Jackie if Robin would have left the door unlocked. She shook her head. "Well," he said, "somebody did."

I said, "I think he killed her."

But she shook her head again. "No, he didn't."

"I could beat it out of him."

"I don't think so. Let me try." And to Phillie, "You don't want cops on this. And you don't want Alex angry."

"I never killed anybody—"

"I know. But you got to tell this right, Phillie. The door was open and you went inside and took the watch and the wallet and Robin's purse. Right?" He nodded. "And then what?"

"I split."

"How?"

"I just walked out."

"No. When Alex woke up the door was bolted. You better tell this straight, Phillie, and then you'll get out of it clean, no police, nothing. But don't buy yourself more trouble."

He thought about this and evidently decided it was reasonable enough. "I went down the fire escape."

"Why?"

"I had to lug the purse, didn't I? Can you see me walking through the lobby with the purse?"

"You're lying, Phillie."

"Look, I swear to God—"

She spoke slowly, patiently, logically. "You would of emptied the purse. You could walk right out, no problem. Instead you locked the door and took the fire escape, and that's always dangerous, going down a fire escape in the middle of the night. You took the purse instead of taking the time to rifle it, which means you were in a hurry, Phillie. Now you better tell it the way it is."

"I heard somebody in the hallway."

"So?"

"So there was a dead girl in the room and I panicked! Who

wouldn't? I wasn't going to get tied into it. You know how they lay it on a junkie. You know the chance you get from them."

"You heard somebody in the hallway, why didn't you wait until they went away?"

"I was nervous. Who had time to think?"

She took a cigarette. I lit it for her. She said, "Phillie, it would all go smoother if you didn't try and hold out. You saw the killer leave that room. You saw him go, and you thought maybe the room was empty and you took a peek inside. You locked the door because you were afraid he was coming back, and when you heard noises in the hallway you went down the fire escape. You were scared bad because you knew what would happen if he found you there. You knew all along Alex didn't kill Robin because you saw the man who did, and that's the only way it makes any sense, Phillie, that's the only way it reads, and now all you have to do is tell me who the man was. You tell us that, Phillie, and you can take your face to a hospital."

"I didn't recognize him."

"Otherwise there's going to be cops. I mean it now. He never has to know who fingered him."

"He'll find out."

"There's trouble if you don't talk, Phillie."

"Every way there's trouble." He worried his broken nose. "Everywhere I look there's always trouble."

"Cop trouble's worse."

"Yeah?" He sighed. "That fucking watch. I shouldn't of taken it, and then I knew better than to sell it. I was gonna throw it away. But then I had to get hungry, a lousy ten bucks, two nickel bags, and look what I bought for it."

"I want a name, Phillie."

"What makes you sure I know him?"

"The way you said you didn't recognize him. Otherwise you would of said you didn't see him. Don't play games with me, Phillie."

"I'm dead. If I tell you, I'm fucking dead."

"You're dead if you don't."

"Beautiful."

"I'm waiting, Phillie."

He looked at her. He said, "Fuck it, I'm dead either way. It was Turk Williams."

Their voices continued. They came at me through air that had gone suddenly thick and heavy.

"That better be the right name, Phillie."

"You know who I mean? The Turkey?"

"I've heard of him."

"The big dealer?"

"Yes."

"Would I cop out on him if he wasn't the one? Be serious, would I pick him? I saw him. I was down the hallway, he never got a look at me, but I saw him. With blood on his hands."

"Then you knew what you'd find in the room."

"Yeah, I guess I did."

"But you went in anyway."

"I was up tight. You been there, you know what it is."

"I know."

"You tell the Turkey where you got it, you know I'm dead."

"We won't tell him."

"I'm dead anyway. You'll put cops on me. The hell, I'm the only witness there is. I'm sitting here and I'm talking to you and my face is a mess and I'm dead."

"Oh, you'll live, Phillie."

"Yeah. Live. Live, yeah."

· 22 ·

I SAID, "I DON'T UNDERSTAND IT. HE WAS MY FRIEND. I KNEW him in prison, I helped him get free. I just talked to him a couple of days ago. He wanted to help me get to Mexico. He thought he owed me a favor."

We were at Jackie's apartment. She had cleaned my cuts with iodine, and now I looked at my battle scars and marveled at myself. I had never fought like that before. How wild I had been, how utterly I had devastated that poor little junkie.

"Jackie, was he telling the truth?"

"He must of been. He would lie, but not give us somebody like Turk Williams. He might make up a name or give us somebody small. But to pin it on Turk, it would have to be the truth."

"You know Turk?"

"I know who he is."

"Didn't I tell you about him?"

"Not his name. Alex, I—"

I stood up, paced the floor. "He had no reason to frame me," I said. "It doesn't make any sense. Unless . . . well, maybe it was something like this. Suppose somebody had something on him, something that would put a lot of pressure on him. So that he had no particular choice. You see what I mean? I don't think anyone could have hired him to frame me, but someone might have blackmailed him into it."

"Maybe."

"What else could it be? Unless Phillie lied—" I thought back to my conversation with Turk, ran it through my mind again. "No," I said, positive. "Phillie wasn't lying. I didn't pay any attention at the time, but Turk was very interested in finding out if I had recognized the killer. He wanted to know what the arm looked like. I remember he asked if it was white or colored, and when I said I didn't know he said something to the effect that I couldn't even say for sure if it was a man or a woman. And he suggested that it might come to me later. He didn't let up until I told him I was sure I would never dig up any more of it." I took a breath. "And then he started telling me how I ought to get out of the country, at least until the air cleared. Phillie wasn't lying. It was Turk. I'm damned if I know why, but it was him."

"Alex—"

"But who put him up to it? That's the question."

She got to her feet. "Alex, I don't see how we can go up against him. I scored off him once but I don't even think he would remember. And he's supposed to carry a gun all the time, you know. Somebody like Phillie is one thing, but to go up against Turk in Harlem—"

"Forget it."

"I suppose I could pretend to make a buy from him. That's what I thought before, but if he knows you—"

I waved the thought aside. "You're missing the point. We don't have to get to him. The buck stops with him, he's the one. He killed Robin, true?"

"Yes, but—"

"And we have evidence. We have a witness, although the doctors will have to put his mouth back together before he can testify. An eyewitness who saw Turk come out of that room with Robin's blood on him. We've got another witness who can establish that Phillie Schapiro had my watch, which marks him on the scene at the time. The police can shake out the rest. We have all we need."

"Then what do we do? Call the police?"

"Exactly."

She thought this over, then began to nod slowly. "Sure," she said. "I never thought of that, isn't that funny? Cops, we spent so much time staying away from them, I never even thought of going to them. Not until we had it all wrapped up with a bow on it."

"But we do."

"Yeah," she said, "I guess we do."

But I didn't call them myself, or wander on down to the nearest precinct house to turn myself in. There had been too much running and hiding of late, too much of disguises and lurking in shadows, too much of being the hunted man. Instead I used Jackie's phone to call Warden Pillion.

"I solved it," I told him. "I know who killed the girl. I can even prove it."

"You're positive, Alex?"

"Yes. I want to surrender to the police, but I want them prepared to listen to me and to put out a pickup order for the killer right away. Can you arrange it?"

"That shouldn't be difficult."

I gave him the address of Jackie's place and some of the details. After I hung up we checked her stash of drugs and made sure the capsules of heroin and the hypodermic needle were not where the police would be likely to stumble upon them. Jackie said it wouldn't be any problem, that homicide cops didn't bother shaking down junkies. I didn't want to take any chances.

And then we sat around and waited. I felt as I have often felt when I have had too little food and too much coffee, excitement bubbling nervously within me, my stomach shaky, my body fidgety, incapable of remaining long in one position. I paced the floor and waited, and then we heard squad cars coming, their sirens wide open, and then the cars pulled up in front and someone rang Jackie's bell.

She went downstairs to let them in. She led them upstairs,

and they came in with guns drawn, and I surrendered with a smile. The soldier suit surprised them somewhat. But they were distinctly hostile at first. I had been a fugitive for a long time, and as far as they were concerned I was just a murderer with a far-out story. They took me to the station house and Jackie came along.

There they put Jackie in one room and led me off to another, and a group of detectives clustered around and kept asking me questions. I answered everything, and I explained just how I knew that Turk Williams was the killer, and how he had done it, and how they could prove it. About halfway through they put out arrest orders for Williams and Schapiro and sent someone to question the roundfaced fence who'd had my watch. Around that time I knew they were ready to believe me, and from that point on we all relaxed. They still didn't like me. As far as they were concerned I should have given myself up Sunday morning and let them take it from there.

"Playing detective like this," one of them said, "all you make is trouble."

"And if I turned myself in right away?"

"We'd have found Williams."

"Sure you would. You had me cold, you wouldn't have looked any further."

"Maybe, maybe not."

"Well," I said, "I like it the way it turned out. I played it your way the first time. Evangeline Grant. And I stood trial and got a life sentence. They'll reverse that when you bring in Williams. Just find out who hired him. That's all."

"We never pegged him as a hired killer—"

"No, and I can't see it that way either. But someone put pressure on him, someone with a reason."

"Any ideas who?"

I thought it over until my head ached. I shook my head. No ideas, none at all.

They fed me, then sat me down again and had me dictate a

formal statement. In the course of this a uniformed cop came in and announced that they had picked up Phillie. "He'll talk," the cop said. "He knows better than to hold out. But somebody sure beat the hell out of him. The doctor's looking at him now." He flashed me a look of the sort that generally gets described as grudging admiration. "But I don't guess he's about to press charges."

I went on with my statement. And I finished it, and they brought Jackie in, and we were all of us sitting around over cups of coffee, when another policeman burst in with news about Turk Williams.

They had surprised him at his Harlem apartment. He said, "Now what's the difficulty, gentlemen? You know the place is always clean and pure." And they said, "A girl named Robin, Turkey. Murder."

And the Turkey went for his gun.

He shot one cop in the arm. Nothing very serious. And they shot him once in the chest and twice in the stomach, and at the moment he was in St. Luke's Hospital with doctors working on him. They didn't expect him to live.

· 23 ·

Jackie and I rode to the hospital in the back seat of a squad car. "He's got to stay alive," I kept saying, over and over. "He's got to talk."

"You're off the hook anyway, Penn. You're clear."

"I've got to know who hired him."

"We'll probably find out. Pick up some of the suspects, sweat 'em a little bit. Amateurs talk."

"But where's the proof? The first murder was years ago."

"There may be a link. If there is, we'll find it."

"He has to talk," I said.

I sat in a waiting room at the hospital and chain-smoked like an expectant father. Jackie kept telling me not to worry, that everything was going to be all right. I worried anyway.

People kept coming in with bulletins. Several times he just about died, and each time the doctors performed some medical miracle and kept him alive. Then around two-thirty one of the detectives came in and sat down across from us. "He's conscious," he said.

"And?"

"He talked. They generally do once they know they're dying. He admits killing the girl." The detective looked suddenly exhausted. "He, uh, wants to talk to you," he told me. "Don't go if you don't want to, it's not necessary, but—"

I got to my feet. Jackie's hand was tugging at my arm. "Don't," she said.

"He wants to talk to me."

"So? He's crazy, Alex. He might—"

"What? He's ninety per cent dead. I want to hear what he has to say."

She let go of my arm. I walked down a corridor and into a room, and there was a bed in it and Turk was on the bed. A bottle was dripping something into his arm. His eyes were closed when I walked in, and I looked at him for a few moments unobserved. His skin was gray, already lifeless.

He opened his eyes, saw me. And smiled. "Fountain," he said. "My man, my man. The Turkey is dying."

"Easy—"

"No harm, man, I don't feel a thing. They got me so shot up with morph and demerol and what-all. I'm just so free and easy. I never knew why all those junkies did it, man, and now I think I do."

"Turk, I—"

"No, let me talk. There's not much time. Oh, baby, why did you have to be there? That's all I want to know. Like you're my man, like you got me out of slam and I owed you, you know? Why did you have to *be* there?"

"What do you mean?"

"Why, with that hooker, man. That Robin. You know, I got a call, where she was, the hotel and the room, and I went down there and who's with her but my man Fountain." He managed a smile. "You shoulda come in with me, man. No chasing 'em around Times Square. Woulda had your pick of nice uptown tail. Anything you wanted, price no object."

"You killed the girl to frame me—"

"*Frame* you?" He sighed heavily. "Baby, I cut that junkie bitch to cut her, dig? I used to sell to that sweet man of hers, that Danny. And then I found out he was dragging down on me, he was stealing and then he was hustling the smack on his own, cutting into my own customers. That little bitch put him up to it. Junkie dreams, you dig?" He started to laugh, but I guess the motion was painful and he stopped. "Junkie dreams. They all think they can sell, and feed themselves on the profits, and they can never stand the hassle, you know. But I couldn't allow that, see. Word gets around and everybody tries, and before you know it a man's sales drop and he gets his whole territory cut out from under him. Can't allow that. So I had to waste Danny—"

"He died of an overdose."

"Funny kind of an OD. That was strychnine, man. I laid two bags of it on him, figured he and Robin would get off together. And don't you know he had to hog both bags himself?" He shook his head. "You just can't trust a junkie, man. He figured to share with his woman, right? But he took it all himself, and I had to go and kill her on my own."

My hands and feet were numb, as though my blood had simply stopped running. I wanted to go away.

"So I had the word out, you know, and I got this call and went to the hotel, and all I had to do was say who I was and she opened the door for me. She thought Danny OD'd, same as you. Never suspected I had any reason to burn her. And I knew she would have a trick with her, but I figured if I had to kill somebody extra it wouldn't be no never mind. But it was *you*, man! I mean, I owed you, and last thing I wanted to do was to put a knife in you."

He stopped abruptly and his eyes went glassy. I thought it was the end. Don't die yet, I thought. More, more. Tell me all of it, make some sense out of it.

"Man, this dying is too much. Feels so funny—"

"Turk—"

"I cut her, see, and I never thought you would open your eyes. So then I got out of there. I had her damn blood all over me and I had to go wash myself clean. Then I was going to get out and go home, but I remembered how you got in trouble the first time, see, and I thought I better do something or you be up against it. I was almost out of the hotel and then I went back upstairs to the room. I was going to haul you out of there and put you someplace else so you wouldn't ever know anything about it. But the door was locked, see, so I knew you was awake—"

"There was a thief in the room. He locked it."

He nodded slowly. "Yeah. Now it fits. I figured you was awake and you'd get out of there on your own, see? So I cut out fast. And here I owed you to begin with, and then the next day I discover it's worse than ever, you didn't get up and you didn't get out and the police are after you. Man, I went out looking for you. And when you called I wanted to give you money, give you my car, anything, just get you out of the country and let everything get cool again. I hate owing anything to anybody. I was born owing nothing to nobody and I wanted to go out the same way, and here I'm going out and still owing you. Ain't that too much?"

"Turk—"

"I knew if they caught you it'd all be up for you, and instead it turns around and it's all up for me. Just too much."

"Turk, the first girl—"

"And me owing you, and all."

"Evangeline Grant—"

"Now if I'd of drug you out of the room right away, or if I waited another couple minutes wiping my hands and that thief was gone by then, why, you never woulda been in it. Both of us, we'd never be in it."

I said, "Evangeline Grant, Turk. The first girl. Five years ago. Who . . . who killed her?"

"And I'm owing you. And never no more chance to make it straight with you, either." He shuddered. "That hurts as bad as dying. Cause all I wanted was a chance to make it straight with us."

"It's straight, Turk."

I hadn't thought he'd be able to hear me, but I guess he did. He did his best to smile, and he said something I couldn't make out, and then he settled back in his bed and died.

They were silent in the waiting room. Jackie, the cops. I walked over to them, and some of them looked at me and others carefully looked away.

"He's dead," I announced, but no one seemed to care.

"He told me everything."

"Well, it clears you completely, Mr. Penn, and—"

"What about the other girl?"

"That was years ago, and—"

"Evangeline Grant—what about her?"

"We don't—"

"Who killed her?"

I stood listening to the echo of my own words in the sterile silent room. Why do we ask such questions? A cop got to his feet. He came over to me, and he laid an infinitely gentle hand upon my shoulder and he spoke very softly, very softly indeed.

He said, "I'm afraid you did, Mr. Penn."

· 24 ·

A LOT HAPPENED AFTER THAT BUT I DO NOT REMEMBER IT VERY well. I moved through it as a ship through fog. There was some police business, and some forms to fill out, and a horde of newspapermen, and flashbulbs popping in my face. That sort of thing. And eventually it stopped and I escaped, and found a bar and had a drink, and then everything slipped away and the days and nights went by. I don't know how many of them there were. Somewhere along the line I got to my bank and took out a lot of cash, so I didn't have to worry about money. I just stayed drunk and the days went by. If I went too long between drinks I thought about things that I did not want to think about, and that was bad, so I stayed drunk.

Until one day or night I looked up from a drink and saw her face. I knew that I recognized her but I could not remember at first just who she was. I couldn't remember.

She said, "Oh, baby, you've been hard to find. You've been so hard to find."

Then I knew who she was. "Jackie," I said. "You're Jackie."

"You better come home with me, Alex."

"Can't go home," I said. "Can't."

"Come on, Alex."

"I'm a dangerous man. Killed a girl. Might hurt you, Jackie."

"You come with me, baby."

I picked up my glass and spilled most of my drink on myself. She was holding my arm, trying to draw me out of that place. The other drinkers were regarding us with appropriate interest.

"Let's go, baby."

"Gotta keep drinking."

"We'll pick up a bottle. There's a liquor store down the street, we'll take a bottle home with us."

"Cause I gotta keep drinking."

"Sure, baby. Come with me, now."

She got me out of there. She picked up a bottle of Scotch at a nearby liquor store and stopped a cab and helped me into it. On the way to her place the motion got to me, and the driver stopped the car so that I could get out long enough to be sick. Then we went to her place, and I was sick again, and she opened the bottle for me and I drank enough of it and passed out.

I went on drinking for about a week. She made sure I took in food along with the liquor, and she had a doctor come by from time to time to give me vitamin shots. During all this time I was something less than a person. Each night she went out to hustle, first waiting until I passed out, then locking me in with a bottle handy in case I woke up before she returned.

Until finally I woke up one morning and didn't want a drink, and knew that I would not want a drink again for a long time. I was sick for that day and most of the next day, but I was done with the drinking, and by the following night I was feeling better again.

"What we do to ourselves," she said. "Jesus, the things we do to ourselves."

"You saved me, Jackie."

"You would of come out of it by yourself sooner or later. I was just afraid you might get in trouble."

"I've never been on that kind of a binge before. It lasted a long time."

"It's over now."

"I hope to God it's over."

"It is, Alex. You had to get it out of your system, and it's out now, and it's over."

"Jackie, I killed that girl."

"I know."

"For a while I tried to tell myself the first one could still be a frame, but I know better. I couldn't sell it to myself, not after Williams confessed. I killed Evangeline Grant."

"I know. I knew it before you did."

"You—"

"As soon as I knew it was the Turkey," she said. "I knew Robin had dealings with him, and I thought about Danny, and I knew it had to be something like that. Either that she worked some kind of a cross on him, or that she sold him out to the cops, set him up for an arrest, something like that. It had to be."

"You knew it all along."

She nodded. "And after he was shot, when they didn't know if he would come to or not, I was praying he would die. All the time that you were hoping he would talk I was praying he'd die with his mouth shut. So you would never know. I fell apart when the cop came out and said he talked. And then let you go to see him. I knew what was coming and I fell apart inside. I tried to stop you—"

I remembered. "I never even thought she could have been killed for private reasons. It never occurred to me."

"Well, you wanted to be innocent, Alex."

"Uh-huh."

She took one of my hands in hers. "Listen to me," she said. "You killed somebody once. You got drunk and you didn't know what you were doing and it happened. All right. You have a temper, Alex. You do. You told me about your sister-in-law, how you were ready to kill her—"

"Anybody would have—"

"And with that fence, Alex, I saw the look on your face.

You were ready to take him apart. You got on top of it and nothing happened, but imagine if you were drunk at the time."

I didn't say anything.

"Or with Phillie, the way you beat up on him. You weren't just trying to frighten him. You just let go." She squeezed my hand. "Look, you have a temper and one time it got away from you. You were drunk and it got loose. But you lived with that for a few years, Alex, and you're free now, and it's over."

"And I'm a killer again."

"You want to write out a label and paste it on your forehead. *Killer*. Listen, you want to know something? I had three abortions. Three. I can't ever have kids. So I'm three killers."

"It's not the same."

"What's the difference?"

"You know the difference."

"Maybe."

"I was going to go back to work," I said. "I was going to become a professor again. I don't feel very professorial right now."

"Maybe you still can."

"Not a chance."

"Well, you can do something."

"What?"

A stretch of silence. Then, "I just wish I knew how to say things better. I know what I want to say but I don't get the words right."

"Go ahead."

She turned away from me. In a small, clear voice she said, "Well, I don't know what good it does either of us, Alex, but I love you. That's all."

In the little bedroom where she had never lain with any man but me I said, "I can't be in very good shape after all that drinking. I may not be much good to you."

"Oh, Alex. Oh, baby."

"How soft you are."

"Baby—"

"How warm."

And afterward, in the warm sweet darkness, I said, "You're not going out tonight. You're staying here."

"Yes."

And neither of us said anything about tomorrow.

She stayed home the next night, and the night after that. But the following night she told me she had to go out for awhile.

"Stay here."

"You know I got to go out."

"I have money."

She started to cry. I didn't know why, and I waited, and she said, "Alex, it's bad enough I have to be a whore. But I won't be *your* whore, I won't do it, I won't take your money and put it in my arm."

"Do you need it that much?"

"You know how I get. You've seen me. You know what I am."

"Could you kick?"

"I don't know."

"You did before."

"Yeah. A few times."

"Could you do it again?"

"Kicking is easy. How many times did you quit smoking? And start up again?"

We tossed it back and forth for a while, and then of course she went out as she had planned, and I wanted a drink for the first time since the binge. But instead I stayed in the apartment and drank coffee. She was gone a few hours. When she came back she went straight into the bathroom and stood under the shower for half an hour. Then she went into the bedroom and took a shot, and then she came out and looked at me and started to cry.

"I don't know," she said. "I just don't know."

"We'll try."

"I just don't know."

"I love you, you know."

"I know it. Otherwise you couldn't stand me."

"We'll try."

"The things we do to ourselves, Alex. The things we do to each other." She slumped on the couch. "I couldn't turn myself off tonight. That's what I always have to do, to turn myself off and just be a machine. I couldn't make it tonight, I thought I was going to be sick. I wanted to die."

"Don't think about it."

"They have this thing called methadone for when you want to kick. It makes it easier. You would have to help me."

"I will."

"Alex, I can't guarantee a thing—"

"We'll try, that's all."

"What happens if I fall down?"

"I pick you up again."

"You won't let go, will you?"

"No. Never."

She only fell down once and she got up right away and stayed on her feet. And after she was past the methadone and the codeine and the thiamine, after she was as clean as doctors could make her, we got out of the city and came here. It's a little town in Montana where you can drink the air and breathe the water, and it is three thousand miles and several hundred years away from Times Square.

We have new names, and if anybody knows who we are they haven't let us know about it. We bought a little diner and live in the three rooms upstairs of it. I do most of the cooking, and seem to have an aptitude for it. Jackie is putting on weight and looks better than ever. We don't make much money, but we don't need much money, either. And when you own a restaurant you never go hungry.

Understand this, it is not all roses. We are not sure that we will make it. Nothing is ever certain. We do not know quite where we are going. But where you are going is less important, I think, than where you are. And still less important is where you have been.